THE BARBER BLUEPRINT

By Aaron VALED Bassett

BarberBlueprint.net

Table of Contents

INTRODUCTION

Forever is a mighty long time… I couldn't see myself being in the game as a barber for over twenty years. I still feel young today, even when a decade of ownership just flew by like an Aston Martin. I guess it could be a blur since I knocked out three studio albums and a slew of mixtapes, then I also got into some legal troubles along the way too. However, barbering has been the focal point of how some people view me on the surface. What we do as professionals isn't all that we are or all we'll ever be. At first, we realize we have a passion; it's exciting to learn it, build up a skill set, gain a following, and then what's next? You may want to continue to grow or feel limited—type cast in one role.

Loyal clients who've been supportive kept me on the court; however, my passion had to be relit in other areas of this industry besides service. Keeping up in the business has been a big issue for many professionals; some never find a way to stay motivated and passionate, and many pros in the game lack exposure to people, places, and things that spark creativity and growth. That unmet hunger for more can lead to depression, anxiety, burnout, or even death. These barber eyes have seen it all; from barbers drinking their own astringent, to others having affairs with their clients(and each other). If I wasn't sharing my perspective on what I've been through, it could lead to many teachable moments dying with me. Truthfully, as a barber, we'll have to keep going with fumes in the tank. We'll have to outwork the competition. We'll have to go above and beyond for people that can leave us for another barber like we are a toxic relationship. Barbers are everywhere nowadays, making the game more competitive than ever. Luckily for you, many of them aren't that good. Most of them live in an average reality and only do the minimum.

Before barbering, I've had two "real" jobs, and both combined for only a total of six months of my life. I had a 'boss,' and I ain't like it. Those jobs were wasting my time and energy, and I knew that lifestyle wasn't for me. It's just been the streets, hustling mixtapes, and this! I'm not job-shaming; simply saying I had other goals in mind, so that you'll get the real time experience of how it happened with me. I learned outside and stacked up wins after taking many losses. Before, I couldn't get haircuts, but now I give haircuts. I didn't go to school for barbering, and now I speak about barbering at schools. If you had pulled up on me ten years ago and told me I'd have a published book on the shelf, I'd think you were on meth! Much about my life was a vision that only I could see. Even with my vision, some events were unforeseeable, and I appreciate it more and more every day.

I wouldn't be here without my family. My mom deserves a great deal of credit for my conditioning. The environment she raised me in is where I got the grit and grind. My father served as a spiritual guide and broadened my worldview beyond the eastside of Buffalo, NY. My Grandmother encouraged me since I was drawing comics and supported me in my most crucial times. This book is dedicated to my family and friends that tolerated my cuts when I was still learning and my loved ones who are no longer with us. I'm proud and thankful for the Fade in Full teams of the past, present, and future; we are helping one another manifest our dreams together. You, the reader, are the true winner, and I thank you for giving this book a fair shot. Hopefully, you won't have to go through all that I went through in this barber game. I hope that my tales of tax advice from Uber drivers, gay barbers, and failed partnerships can inspire you to start, push you to get those clients, and eventually build your own legacy. I look forward to seeing you make it happen!

HISTORY AND GROWTH

"History is dependent on the new generation to write a new chapter." - Lamelo Ball

Let there be light

The Barber Game has been here since the first man wanted a haircut. How they did it in prehistoric times may shock us. Before spray enhancements and gold trimmers, the cavemen needed haircuts to post selfies. While Eve ate the forbidden fruit, God blessed Adam with a groomed beard. Barbering dates back an extensive 7000 years ago to Egyptians by using shells and sharp objects to get the job done. Shaving and hair dressing, not yet a specialized skill, was practiced with a list of other services like repairing wounds, surgery, and dentistry throughout early time. Some say Barbers were more advanced then, but I disagree. By my standards, barbers shouldn't do everything, because it's like doing nothing at all. You wouldn't get a haircut from a surgeon or a root canal in a Barbershop. Maybe hair was an afterthought.

Who do we credit for the evolution of hair and style? Who'd be the quintessential Michael Jordan or Thomas Edison of it? Names come to mind like Madam CJ Walker, who revolutionized hair straightening and products, or Nikola Bizumic, who's credited with inventing the manual hair clipper. Yet, they don't get the flowers like the Elon Musks or Grandmaster Cazs of the world. A 64B industry with no Mount Rushmore. Even local legends and influencers from my hood like Big Jay, Sean Thompson, or Jimmy Stanfield don't get the credit they deserve. When asking the new generation of Barbers, they'll mention Chris Bosio, 360 Jeezy, and others who've made waves in the information age. I've met Barbers around the world who aren't connected or have the same teachings, yet one common theme stands out. We aren't united, respected, or celebrated for all that we've contributed to society. Behind every polarized leader, award-winning celebrity, or hard-working person stands a Barber. Think about it; you have thousands of networks, award shows, reality shows, and sitcoms without Barbers as the focal point. Barbers don't even get mentioned in acceptance speeches, inaugurations, or wedding toasts. We have Ice Cube's trilogy of Barbershop movies, and it ends there. Even as an artist, I've yet to make a full song about my shop and how ill I am as a Barber. Look behind closed doors at any given shop, and you'll find Barbers who think they're the best, but they aren't that good, and some who actually should be recognized for their ability, stuck behind their chair with a wealth of knowledge dying there. If you're reading this, you probably feel like me. The world has evolved faster than ever with tech, and Barbers just got wireless clippers and booking apps.

This life chose me

The fact that I grew up in an east-side housing project didn't make my haircut a priority. With limited resources, my family focused on more pressing needs like food and housing. But, like many inner-city millennials in the 80s, I was captivated by the emerging styles and fashion of hip-hop culture. A new type of music, art, expression, and language was cultivated, and fashion trends of the past were replaced with new icons like Jordans, Shelltoe Addias, Rope Chains, Dapper Dan Suits, Cazal Frames, and the Hi Top Fade. It was a haircut I had always wanted but couldn't have. My grandfather, who has been a barber for decades, was unable to figure out how to create this style. My mother's attempts hurt; it took hours and resulted in a look resembling a tiny black fez on top of a basketball. It was a source of embarrassment and ridicule from students and teachers, and at just six years old, I started skipping school to avoid the emotional stress. But that pain led to a purpose for me.

Just do it

Fixing my own hair became a routine by third grade. My ability to draw and my interest in art was all that made me socially accepted in class. Oftentimes, I'd accompany a friend to the barber shop when his mom sent him in for haircuts, sit quietly, and watch the barbers work while wearing a hat. I tried the techniques on my own with no guidance, and after hours in the bathroom mirror, the results were scars from disposable razors, lopsided fades, or streaky all even cuts.

By fifth grade, I lived with my grandmother, and she took me to a shop on Wednesdays to see a man named Sonny. I probably got on his nerves while watching his every move and asking a million questions. My neck and sides had never been so smooth; the lines were symmetric, a blurry blend, and the top so flat! I fell in love with my reflection, and it was a much needed confidence boost during an uncertain time. He remained my barber while I was living with my grandmother. Other living situations subsequently lead to me having to cut my own hair again. My skills improved, and some of the people in the hood were paying me once I set up shop on my mom's front porch.

In the 90s, people were outside more, and the neighborhood was action-packed. So if I wasn't giving a cut, my friends and I would catch a vibe listening to music or playing street football. $5 cuts and $2 shape-ups bought clippers, school clothes and kept me out of trouble for a while. Although I didn't know the fundamentals of sanitation or cutting techniques, but as at that time, my end result was fair for a kid cutting hair. I also stole a few clients with my low price and accessibility. For instance, someone was on my block getting money, the competition was fierce out there, and leaving the street too long for a haircut meant missing an opportunity to hit a lick. One of the most powerful and respected guys would only get cuts from me at my mom's house even after I made it to the shop. He could've easily paid whatever a cut cost, yet he'd give me $30 or $50 for a cut and some hand-me-down clothes too. Words spread about the kid cutting hair on the porch, and a barber shop around the corner became interested.

Get Faded was a fairly new barbershop in 1999, and walking in to meet them for the first time was intimidating. I was 16 and not too far from watching Nicktoons—a porch barber amongst grown men. I spoke to the owner, Brian, who invited me through a guy on my street named Peanut. It seemed as if I already had the job when I walked in because he wanted me to come right back with my clippers. The shop sat on a corner a few blocks down from where I lived near housing projects where I'd never walk alone back then. The barber chairs were average, individual lights brightened up the space above large mirrors and fake marble countertops with hooks to hang clippers. Waiting chairs lined the windows with bars to secure the premises. A quick convo with Brian, and I was plugging up my tools. My setup was basic; cheap Oster adjustable clippers and a pair of Wahl trimmers I scored for $40 at the Chinese hair supply store. My blades were a little rusty, my shears were probably best for paper, my guards and combs missed their teeth, and all of this sat on a towel from home, next to a bottle of clear alcohol and disinfectant spray. My workspace was in the middle chair, and I sat around feeling like all eyes were on me. At times, I felt pressure that caused my hands to shake and my voice to crack while answering to adults that had high expectations for their hair. Some would micromanage me. Because they knew that I was a teen starting out.

I was left to struggle on cuts before the senior of the group, a barber named Bam, showed me how to actually fade with a pair of Andis Masters. I had never seen that clipper before working there. He explained how the settings on the adjustable work, and showed me how to adjust blades and lineups with the trimmer of that era; The Andis T-Outliner. Bam had an arsenal, two of every clipper & trimmer, all types of sprays, and drawings on poster boards of his designs for customers to pick from. He was a heavy hitter there, servicing the older folks, kids and didn't take many breaks. A guy closer to my age, named Toumani, took me under his wing. I learned a lot from him outside of cutting hair, and we'd be hanging out and cracking jokes during my $10 weeks. I developed most of my early style from watching and mimicking him. My booth rent was $50, cuts were $10, and shape-ups were $5. My rent was half of what the full timers were paying since I was only available after school and Saturdays. Convincing my mom to let me work there was a challenge, so most days, I went there straight from school and pretty much stayed there, making it home by 10 pm most nights. Get Faded drafted me, and I seized the opportunity.

The shop was where I could control my own destiny and experience some adulthood. My peer group was in the streets or had part time jobs. I had a mix of both worlds; a job on my own terms, and freedom that allowed me to be creative, absorb my culture, and meet people that didn't live on my street. I took pride in having role models within my first team. They weren't quite Dr. Martin Luther King Jr, but they weren't David Koresh either. Being embraced by the shop kept me in the loop, not too deep in the streets, and allowed me to contribute at home for a while. The unprofessionalism and tension were what I thought was normal for a shop—a far cry from the old school vibes of Sonny's Barbershop with my grandma.

In Get Faded, we blasted rap music, smoked trees, smoked baby mamas, and occasionally opened up to no electricity or heat! Still, my first impression of working in a shop challenged me to be a quick and competitive barber. Staying there and always being there was my first key to success. Listening and watching was how I learned customer service, and minding my business kept me out of petty beef and disputes. Paying my rent early guaranteed my spot, and being a familiar face there made it easy for people to trust me when I moved on to different shops.

Adopting a DIY mindset helped me survive, learn new skills, and build a reputation as a Barber in my neighborhood. My barbershop leadership roles helped me rise from a lower status to a sense of freedom. Finding our purpose in life means designing the best version of ourselves and making a lasting impact. Although barbering wasn't my lifelong dream, I'm forever thankful it found me. This art has enabled me to create a quality life, empower the next generation, service athletes, entertainers, and friends while traveling the world.

Fade in Full, founded by me in 2015, has grown into one of the most reputable barber shops in Buffalo, New York. We have the support of our city, loyal clients, and a dedicated team. Since 2016, Mr. Wes has contributed to our growth. We met through a mutual contact at Barber School, and Mr Wes has been chopping since 1984! He purchased a pair of clippers with paper route money, and practiced on himself for a year with only one clipper for the takedown, blend, and edge up. His professional experience was from part time at a shop in Memphis. Returning to Buffalo led him to settle down with his wife, who's been supportive and encouraging him to pursue his dreams of being a full time Barber. He and I hit it off pretty fast with a mutual love for music, and he was locked in after we talked. His wisdom, consistency, and promotion in the local newspapers, coupled with his patience in guiding our interns and upcoming barbers are priceless. Having him around keeps barbers, clients, and me on point. In the beginning, we bootstrapped everything; we weren't always clean and family friendly. Along the line, we learned much about ourselves and how our personal decisions reflect how we conduct business.

Our first location was a 700 square foot space with no break room, water damage on the floors, a lingering food odor from a neighboring business, and daily drama. Yes, different daily dramas like a freestyle rap battle which resulted in two kids putting hands and feet on a grown man on Friday evening and him coming back looking to retaliate several times the following Saturday. Another one was about a drunk meat man who came through selling us steaks, shrimp, and frozen chicken wings that thawed out and really were chicken backs! Also, a barber that claimed to be from Miami and was a con artist that ran off on the plug, then another guy packed up in the middle of the night and left us with no explanation. Our shop was hot in the summer, cold in the winter, and relentless street smarts kept the dream alive.

We offer a comfortable work environment for great barbers following the tension and hostility within those walls. Notable names like Vega, Meg, Kyle, Rullan, and Dom, who are in the Fade in Full Hall of Fame, can attest to the changes in our culture. We have alumni who invested their time and effort and have done amazing things like opening up shops. It's been a pleasure to work with the more recent members as well, like Deez, Pat, Regg, and Lex. They arrived during our most trailblazing years and have fueled our growth since we relocated to Elmwood Village, an affluent area of Western New York known for its boutiques, restaurants, and attractions.

As an apprentice, I worked in seven shops before owning my own, and the lessons were caught more than taught. I'd love to know the amount of value this book brings you because I wish I had it 20 years ago. If you're reading this, it's likely you have a passion and drive that motivates you. Do you wanna get in the game? Open a shop or more locations? Looking to be an educator? Are you burnt out and need the fire relit? Or are you dreaming of manufacturing the world's first smart clipper? Whatever you wanna do, it's possible, and I aim to help you find your way to it.

WHY WE DO THIS

"The two most important days in life are the day you are born and the day you discover the reason why." – Mark Twain

You gon get this work

For most, work is defined by the skills required to do it, but the why behind it is what keeps us motivated. Why do you want to be a Barber? You probably get this question every day. Maybe you know, maybe you're unsure. Do you love to see the reaction when you hand your client the mirror? Do you enjoy the freedom of earning income by controlling your destiny? Do you value the relationships you can form with clients?

How you cut hair and why you cut hair are fundamentally different things. I believe we've found a balance at Fade in Full. We have the inspiration to pursue something more in life, the motivation to do it, the education on what to do, and the automation of systems and processes to execute. We're supportive of one another. Mr

11

Wes could have split and jumped ship when I was going through tough times. Driving me home some nights while I didn't have a car had to be annoying. We've had barbers who needed a place to stay that lived in my crib rent-free until they could get back on their feet. We were able to raise money to help two barbers who were hurt in a car crash .

Recently, we offered to take turns driving one of our barbers to and from work. When you believe in us, we believe in you. When times get rough, we think about how to overcome it, and we consider why it's important to do so. Most Barbers have a lot in common besides the skill of grooming. There's a certain cloth we're cut from. Making it from that first cut to a license and into a shop shows us we have what it takes to stay the course and learn a skill. Once we learn the skill, we learn from one another. We spend time together, share similar challenges, and we execute as a team. Some of us have more than just the skill of styling the hair and servicing the client. There is a type of charisma, charm, and wit barbers acquire by being a part of a shop. There is a network of professionals you have access to. Even the Barber in a tense shop gains intuition.

We bring out the best in one another! We help one another eat for the greater good when we remain true to the game. I've lived through the evolution of "every man for himself," try barbershops to learn team building and business here. Currently, our knowledge is decentralized with weekly meetings, team activities, ideas from our clients, and newsletters. I have dedicated my life to our growth. Everyone who succeeds here is worth all that we've sacrificed to do so, and I hope you will get value here too. Embarking on a new path in life is often fueled by a deep sense of motivation. For those interested in the art of barbering, this motivation ignites a fire within, pushing them to explore the world of clippers, shears, and fades. In this chapter, we delve into the initial stages of the barber journey, where the seed of passion is planted and begins to grow. From expressing interest to taking the first steps, let's explore the exhilarating world of starting a career in barbering.

In the beginning, there was a spark. An interest that catches your attention and guides you towards barbering. You may find yourself mesmerized by a well-groomed haircut or inspired by the transformative power of a fresh fade. You could have a barber friend who is making good money while enjoying the freedom of self-employment. Once you act on that curiosity, you embark on your journey. You gather your courage, set aside doubts, and take that first step. It may be enrolling in a barbering program, signing up for an apprenticeship, or simply deciding to dive headfirst into the world of clippers. Whatever path you choose, it marks the beginning of an exciting adventure. Like anything you try for the first time, it's not gonna be the greatest. Try to take a picture of your first cut to keep as a reference for your progress later. I wish I could see some of the cuts I did early on to see how much my skills have evolved over time.

In the early stages, you realize that guidance from seasoned professionals is priceless, so seeking advice from experienced barbers becomes a crucial part of your development. Whether it's attending industry events, reaching out to established barbers, or joining online communities, it's best to actively seek wisdom and insight to accelerate your growth. Use your best judgment on who to seek advice from. I've known many barbers throughout my time and taken on some of their habits and techniques for better or worse.

One of the first milestones on your journey is cutting the hair of your family and friends. This is where you put your skills into practice, honing your techniques while building trust with loved ones. The satisfaction of seeing their smiles and the confidence they have after a successful cut fuels your passion and affirms your decision to pursue this. Usually, they are quite easy on you since you are just starting. My grandfathers were great for me starting off. They didn't need much detail since they were already bald on top. Mostly I was getting reps for takedowns and working on my lines with them. I had to turn it up when I started cutting hair for people on the street. The hustlers on the block were in my mom's basement twice a week, keeping those lines and blends tight with me. The fact that they trusted me with their hair, even with my little experience, was a confidence booster for me as well; an opportunity I couldn't afford to squander away. Once you have some recurring clients, it's confirmation you're on your way.

In this digital age, learning has become limitless. Aspiring barbers have online resources and can immerse themselves in the vast ocean of barber videos. I had to be actually "in a shop" to watch a haircut and was limited to my city. Hours are spent studying expert techniques, observing different styles, and gaining inspiration from talented barbers worldwide today. These videos become a constant companion, an endless well of knowledge that fuels your growth and nurtures your artistic vision. I'd even suggest making some content while starting off as well to document your journey. We all love a great success story. If indeed you are, feel free to message me and tag me. I wanna see your work!

The motivation stage of the barber journey is an exhilarating time filled with curiosity, exploration, and self-discovery. It's a period where initial interests evolve into concrete steps, and the foundations of your career begin to take shape. As you dive into the barbering world, the fire of motivation continues to burn red hot, propelling you forward towards the next chapter of your journey.

THIS IS HOW WE DO

Fundamentals

Most barbers start with a solid understanding of fundamentals. This stage is the pursuit of knowledge about cutting techniques, hair types, facial structures, and tools. As an aspiring barber, you may devote your time to studying the intricacies like clipper control, shear work, blending, and creating precise lines. During this time, you must build a strong base of technical skills that will serve as the foundation for your career. Too often, I've seen barbers look at the hair aimlessly with no end goal or just cutting one side during a takedown and jumping over to the opposite side with no formula. The basics of cutting hair with clippers should be easy to understand like vacuuming a rug or cutting grass. There are even a few seasoned vets that may need a refresh on the fundamentals. It will take practice but don't skip this. Learn the basics immediately so you don't hurt anyone or your career before it starts.

Late Registration

Formal education at a barber/cosmetology school is a popular and safe route for aspiring barbers. A reputable program provides a structured curriculum, expert instructors, and a supportive learning environment. Writing this as a Master that took the apprentice route, I can confidently say the school barbers had an edge on me and I learned a lot from them. In school, you get an educational experience that covers theory, hands-on practice, and exposure to diverse hairstyles and grooming trends. It's an opportunity to refine those techniques, gain valuable feedback, and connect with fellow students who share your passion.

Through the Fire

For those who prefer a more hands-on approach and learning in a real-world setting, becoming an apprentice is an alternative path that throws you right in the fire. A good apprenticeship offers a learning experience under the guidance of a seasoned barber. All apprenticeships aren't created equal. Some barbershops may charge for their time, knowledge, and access to their customers. An owner who is also a barber may be busy serving their own clients, leaving you to fend for yourself. However, working side by side with a mentor will help you gain practical knowledge, learn industry insights, and get reps through practical application. The apprentice journey instills a deep sense of camaraderie within a team environment. It builds character, relationships and encourages a strong work ethic, dedication, and perseverance. Remove fear and doubt going into an apprenticeship and embrace the experience. It may be easy to lose focus around barbers who are comfortable in the shop atmosphere.

Choices

Throughout the education journey, aspiring barbers face many concerns and much to consider. One of the primary concerns is the allocation of your resources: money, energy, attention, and time. Attending barber school most likely requires a financial investment, yet it offers a structured and fast path to acquiring the necessary skills and license. On the other hand, pursuing an apprenticeship may require more time and effort, but it provides hands-on experience, personalized guidance and access to customers. Choosing your educational path also involves considering your learning preferences. Do you like school? Are you dedicated to the craft enough to sit through class? Financial constraints aren't as astronomical as higher education; however still not cheap. You should also ponder whether or not you can sit in a shop and possibly be making no money for months while you "learn".

What are your career goals? Each route has its advantages and challenges, and it's essential to weigh these factors to make an informed decision that aligns with your aspirations. You're blessed to have these options to ponder on today. Some experienced barbers reading this may have only had one path to mastery. Whether through formal education or apprenticeships, this path offers unique opportunities for growth, self-discovery, and professional development. As you allocate your resources and embark on your chosen route, I'm sure you'll lay a solid foundation for a successful career.

Inspiration

When you're on the journey to becoming a barber, finding inspiration is really important. Discover what you love to know and what fuels and drives you. Make connections with experienced Barbers that have your best interests at heart. Learn how to meet customers' expectations. The exciting phase of inspiration is between learning the craft and executing based on what you now know. We have to discuss finding the right shop or salon and why making friends with experienced Barbers is important. It's a decision that leads you to getting lots of clients or wasting your talents away in a dead end shop.

The G Spot

Finding the perfect shop or salon is a big deal in your career. It's where you start to become a professional and find a place where you belong. While you search for the right spot, think about things like the atmosphere, the people who go there, and how it can help you grow. You want to work in a place that lets your creativity shine and where experienced barbers can teach you new things. Any place will have a range of personalities and goals. The actual shop has a life cycle of its own. In a new and upcoming shop, the staff and owner may share a passion and be more united, which can keep the creativity and imaginative vibes at an all-time high. Expect to spend a ton of time in a new shop. The experience you gain from helping to build a shop can yield some career-defining results. Mr Wes is a great example of that for me. Over the years, he's become a running mate and a builder of sorts. He's been my eyes and ears when I needed a break, and for that, he's the first I'd offer equity to, run ideas by, or tap on to handle an admin task for me because he witnessed all of our systems firsthand, knows the goals of the shop and still has the drive from day one. This is a great opportunity for you to build a career and rise up the ranks contingent upon your contribution to your shop's success. However, if you don't have grandiose goals of ownership or a higher-up position, you can be plugged into a shop with an existing system of operations and a track record of success. Going to a shop where you have some form of guaranteed income upon arrival is great for your quality of life and career. Keep in mind that wherever you decide to go, there will be a difference between the shop's clients and your clients. Arriving at a shop that is already rolling gives you exposure, and since they are providing an experience already, you have to uphold those quality standards. If you leave, those people may stay, so be mindful of whether or not your personal goals can thrive within a team-like culture.

Lovers and Friends

In a busy barbershop or salon, you have a great chance to learn from experienced barbers who have been doing this for a while. Making friends with these experts is super helpful for your own growth. They can be like mentors, showing you the tricks of the trade and giving you great advice. They'll teach you how to make haircuts look amazing, take care of clients, and make them happy. You have to pay attention though. I know this may be obvious to some and irrelevant to most. Just because you are sitting around inside a shop doesn't mean you should just be catching

21

up on Netflix and music videos. Take advantage of a seasoned vet within arms reach. Don't let those years of experience go to waste. You will only go as far as your network and decisions. Strive to build lasting relationships with good barbers and quality clients. You never know when you will need some assistance later on. Brushing this off has left some barbers out in the poor house with nowhere to turn to for advice.

Customers' Expectations

It's really important to satisfy your customers. Understanding what they want, listening carefully, and talking with them in a way that makes them feel comfortable. Each person who sits in your chair has their own style and preferences. They trust you to give them a great haircut and to be a good listener. By doing this, you'll build trust and make them want to come back to you. Seasoned barbers become a master of both conversation and actual service. We can't teach personality. Your interest, character, and integrity play a part in who you attract.

I've been through many different phases, environments and people. One thing for sure that will definitely help your career is being on time. I can't stress this enough. Value your time so your clients can follow your lead. Be at the shop when you say you will be there, and be mindful of your cutting speed to book your appointments accordingly. We'll dive into different types of customers and how to fulfill their requests. Expect the unexpected with customer expectations, stay consistent and communicate with them.

Getting Clients

Having a lot of clients is a big part of being a successful barber. To get clients, you need to be creative and use different strategies. Obviously, you can use social media, ask happy customers to tell their friends, go to events where you can meet new people, and be active in your community. When you do a great job and make your clients happy, they will tell others about you, and more people will want to come to you for haircuts. There will be waves during your career. Sometimes you might be overwhelmed, so know how to say no to some so you can say yes to your longevity. You want a steady flow of good, loyal and supportive clients. People that treat you like a slave or as if you need them more than they need you are not good. Eventually, you will make it to a level of freedom where you can filter through who is best for you and your career.

The stage of inspiration is really important for barbers. It's a time when you explore, make connections, and grow. By finding the right shop or salon, making friends with experienced barbers, meeting customer" expectations, and getting lots of clients, yo"re setting yourself up for a successful career. Embrace the opportunities that come your way, keep learning, and let your love for barbering guide you to becoming the best you can be.

Applying What You've Learned

It's important to apply the techniques and knowledge you gained during your education in addition to the natural instincts you've learned throughout life. Here is where you get to show off your skills and creativity. Each haircut is like a canvas, and you are the artist. You'll use your training to give your clients the best haircut possible, paying attention to details and ensuring they feel confident and satisfied when leaving. Experienced barbers have the ability to keep the fundamentals and conversation on cruise control, while the newer barbers may focus on one or the other. Confidence in your skill level and being honest about it before starting a cut with a customer may ease tension with them during the difficult cut. Most people think I'm joking with them when I tell them they got me under pressure with a cut. I still have to tap into my fundamentals on some cuts and ask for help if I'm inexperienced with a certain skill set. No matter what level you are, you will always apply what you learned.

Doing It Your Way

While it's essential to learn the basics, as you gain experience, you'll develop your own style and techniques. Don't be afraid to think outside the box and put your personal touch into your work. Whether it's a unique fade or a signature hairstyle, doing it your way sets you apart from other barbers and helps you create your own identity in the industry. Doing it your way is beautiful when it's a proven success. There may be some mistakes or errors on the way to your way. Don't get discouraged or bent out of shape. Any barber on this earth that claims their way was the only way from day one must be drug tested. There is nothing wrong with taking a little inspiration from here and some style from there. How you apply it to you and put your twist on it is what makes it your own.

Reaching a Level of Status

As you continue to grow as a barber, you'll have the opportunity to reach a level of status in your profession. This means becoming well-known and respected for your skills and professionalism. It takes time and dedication to build a reputation, but by consistently delivering exceptional haircuts and providing excellent customer service, you'll earn the trust and loyalty of your clients. Word-of-mouth referrals and positive reviews will help you establish yourself as a reputable barber in your community. The stage of instruction is an exciting phase in your barbering journey. It's a time to showcase your skills, embrace your unique style, and work towards reaching a level of status in the industry. Remember to always apply what you've learned, continue to develop your own techniques, and strive for excellence in every haircut. By doing so, you'll pave the way for a successful and fulfilling career as a barber.

MYTHS IN THE BARBER GAME

1. **All shops run on booth rent.**

   While booth rent is a popular business model for Barbershops, it's not the only one. Some shops have a traditional hourly wage model, Commission model, hybrid, or franchise model. Whatever the owner wants to do is their decision, and they should consider all factors like operating expenses, compensation for workers, shop culture, and long term vision before choosing a business model.

2. **Barbers think their s*** don't stink.**

   If you've been asked to leave, fired, or relieved of your duties at a Barbershop, then you stunk! Get your act together and your affairs in order. If nobody wants to work with you, then do your hair at home, in a mobile truck or a suite. The funny thing about this one is we had a barber who wasn't taking showers; smh…

3. **Charging lower prices is the best way to attract people**
Low prices may bring more people, yes. What about the quality of these people, the perception of your service, and the wear and tear on your energy and time?! Not to mention your profits!!! If you live by the price, you'll die by the price, and you better be fast too! Most customers know cheap and fast is never good.

4. **Selling drugs and cutting hair at the same time builds career/ Clientele**
If you believe this, you're reading the wrong book, fam.

5. **All barbers can cut all types of hair.**
All barbers don't have the same skill set or expertise. It's best to specialize first, in my opinion. Focus on your strengths and master your fundamentals before you go off the deep end, trying every style for money inside a shop. It's good to be knowledgeable and skilled with all hair types. Building a strong client base off of what you're good at first is where you will grow in the beginning and continue learning in your free time.

6. **All barbers are good with kids.**
Not true! Some don't have the patience to interact with children or the experience to give them a quality style without making it painful and scary. Some may be creepy

with the moms too. Yeah, that's a thing... Being able to cut kids will build a loyal base and fulfill any commitment you have to uplift your community because you will be a role model to the youth if you're a part of their life.

7. **The barbershop owner is the best barber in the shop**
While some owners may have skill and experience, that doesn't necessarily make them the best in the shop. An owner of a shop should manage and ensure the shop's overall success.

8. **Women can't cut guys' hair.**
Women can definitely cut men's. Some of them are killing it more than some dudes out here!

9. **Women can't go to Barbers.**
Women can for sure get cuts in a Barbershop. Barbers cater to both men and women depending on the service, and it should be no issue for anyone to get what they need if the shop can provide the style.

10. **Barbers can't dye hair.**
Barbers that attend school are trained and licensed to provide hair coloring services. These days shops are offering it too. You'd be surprised who's getting dyed. Or better yet, who's doing the dying...

11. **Enhancements make a good haircut.**

Enhancements are meant to enhance, not to make the entire haircut. The actual cut should be good before you start spraying stuff on people. God forbid it's a hot day, and your client goes to play basketball; you don't want their edge up leaking all over the court.

12. White people can't cut coarse hair.

This was a myth that was dispelled for me once I began to leave my neighborhood. Although there are Barbers that aren't able to do all hair types, yet many can. You'd be surprised how well other races and cultures can do your hair.

13. Names of haircuts may mean different things in different places/regions

A Fade in Philly may mean a Taper in St Louis, and if you go to France and ask for a Fade they may not know what you're talking about at all. Pictures are the universal language in the communication of hairstyles to know for sure what your client is looking for.

14. Barbering is a cash business.

Barbering hasn't been a cash business since we've had devices that read cards for smartphones. While all shops haven't implemented card processing into their shops, they may have atm or the individual barbers can use an app to read cards. Having a bank account and accepting debit and credit makes managing funds so much easier.

15. Weekends are the only busy days/times.

Any day of the week may be a sleeper. The day before a holiday can be busy. A week of graduation or prom can be busy. Concert nights or big events like a wedding can increase business. Don't just only be laser-focused on only the weekends.

16. Barbershops are closed on Sunday & Monday.

Nowadays there are shops open seven days a week.

17. Barbers can't cut long hair.

Barbers are able to learn faster and have access to more knowledge these days. Most barbers with experience can cut long hair.

18. Barbers make a lot of money.

There are plenty of barbers that love this game more than I do. You may be one of them. I've met Barbers that have absolutely no passion for the craft and come in and make a killing here. We're all going to make 'some' money. Making a lot of money depends on your ability to sell yourself and your work ethic. All barbers don't make a lot of money. Barbers that are consistent make the most money.

WHY BARBERS DON'T MAKE IT

1. Speed through Class, Exams, and Haircuts

Barbers shouldn't speed through haircuts, classes, and exams because it's important to have a thorough understanding and mastery of the techniques, tools, and safety measures involved in providing haircuts. Rushing through the learning process leads to mistakes and subpar results, which can harm the reputation of the barber and the shop. It's also important to understand the anatomy and physiology of the hair and scalp, as well as the different hair types and textures, to provide personalized and professional services to clients. By learning and perfecting skills, barbers can provide a higher level of service, build a loyal clientele, and establish a successful career in the industry.

2. Doesn't listen to what the client wants

33

As a barber, it's important to listen to what the client wants because it shows you value their input and preferences, and it also helps ensure you deliver a haircut that they will be happy with. When a barber takes the time to listen to what the client wants, it can help build a positive relationship and increase the likelihood of repeat business. Additionally, by understanding the client's needs and preferences, you can tailor your cutting techniques and style to suit their unique hair type, facial structure, and desired outcome. Ultimately, listening to what the client wants is essential for providing excellent customer service and ensuring the success of your business.

3. **Dirty hands**

A barber's clean hands and hygienic appearance are important for several reasons. It shows the barber's professionalism and respect for their clients. If a barber has dirty hands, it can create a negative first impression and make clients feel uneasy about the grooming process. Cleanliness is a critical aspect of barbering to prevent the spread of germs and bacteria. This is especially important when it comes to haircuts, as the barber is working in close proximity to the client's face skin. Smelling like weed smoke, cigarettes, or body odor can also create unpleasant experiences for clients, resulting in a loss of business. It's important for barbers to maintain high standards of personal hygiene to provide a positive experience for clients and maintain the profession's integrity.

4. Late for Appointments

Being punctual is an important aspect of professionalism and customer service in any business, including barbering. When a barber is consistently late for appointments, it reflects poorly on the shop and can result in frustration and dissatisfaction for clients. Additionally, running behind schedule can disrupt the flow of the day, causing further delays and potentially leading to missed appointments or loss of business. Being prompt and reliable builds trust with clients and demonstrates respect for their time and needs, which can help to foster a loyal customer base and contribute to the success of the business.

5. Unprofessional

It's important for a barber to maintain a professional demeanor because it sets the tone for the client experience and can impact the reputation of the barbershop. Being unprofessional, such as using inappropriate language, engaging in unprofessional behavior, or not being dressed appropriately, can make clients feel uncomfortable and less likely to return. It can also create a negative perception of the barber and the barbershop, potentially impacting business and damaging the barber's personal brand. In the barbering industry, professionalism is highly valued and helps build trust and credibility with clients.

6. Bad Habits and Substance Abuse

Bad habits or substance abuse can significantly impact a barber's professional and personal life. Substance abuse can impair a barber's ability to provide safe, effective, and efficient haircuts, negatively affect their judgment and communication with clients, and create a hazardous work environment. Additionally, it can lead to decreased motivation, decreased productivity, increased absenteeism, and a decline in reputation and clientele.

A barber should seek help and support from friends, family, colleagues, or organizations like substance abuse treatment centers or support groups to improve. Additionally, they can seek professional counseling, participate in a 12-step program, and engage in healthy habits like exercise and healthy eating to maintain their mental and physical health. It's also important to establish clear boundaries and prioritize self-care and stress-management techniques. Making a commitment to maintaining sobriety and professional behavior can help a barber build a successful and fulfilling career in the barbering industry.

7. Can't communicate or doesn't work well with people

A barber who lacks communication skills will struggle to build up clientele. A barber should be friendly and approachable. Improve these skills by actively listening to clients and co-workers. Practice empathy, take public speaking courses, get therapy, and do whatever needs to be done to improve this. Clients will take their business elsewhere or choose another barber in your shop who's easier to deal with than you. It's not about bending over backward for people. It's about not coming off as a weirdo, socially awkward person, or too intimidating. Be open-minded, flexible and remember that this is a social business. Learn the ability to reason and how to deal with many different personalities, and you'll go far in this game.

8. Doesn't evolve with the game

It's challenging for a barber to have a successful career if they never adapt to changes in the industry, like new styles and trends, updated techniques, and new tech. Staying current with developments can help a barber remain relevant and in demand, and can also help them expand their skill set and grow. To evolve with the times, attend workshops, conferences, and classes to stay up-to-date. Do the research and stay informed, and more importantly, stay hungry. Make sure your continual learning and improvement never ends, or you'll lose your spot to the new improved version of you years down the line.

9. Doesn't continue learning

Continual learning is essential to have a successful career. Improving your skills and staying motivated will make you a sought-after barber. As a barber, you are self-employed and essentially run your own personal business. Continual learning can also mean seeking skills that serve your career beyond your services. Learning to promote, attract, and stay afloat during slow times will separate you from the pack.

10. Doesn't have the support system offered at Fade in Full

Have you ever seen The Last Dance? Great! We want to bring that same camaraderie and championship team effort to the Barber Game, where everyone can have Micheal Jordan-level success. We aim to empower our barbers to build a fulfilling career in grooming with culture, quality customer experience, and teamwork.

BOOTH RENT VS COMMISSION

This debate gets pretty heated. I've seen shop owners have some intense discussions over this topic here. As you know, I've been molded and groomed in a booth rent shop all of my career as a Barber, so my only commission experience comes from being an owner of a shop.I'd like to share some of the differences between each choice to guide you towards which type of shop works best for you.

Booth Rent

In this model, barbers rent a space from a shop and in most cases, operate however they see fit (within shop rules). The barber takes on all of the responsibility for the upkeep of the space they pay for. The rent can be monthly or weekly based on the lease agreement between the professional and the shop. The barber is an independent contractor. One of the pros most barbers love about this is the freedom to control their own schedule services and clients. Basically, the barber paying a booth rent is operating a self employed business within the shop. They keep all of their revenue beside the rent and handle all of their own personal expenses, such as supplies, marketing and reputation management. Booth renters have the potential to earn more income based on volume and may have a key to the shop based on trust and professionalism. This model provides little to no incentive for the owner to support the renter in any way outside of their lease agreement. A shop full of renters creates a competitive space that can be cutthroat depending on the shop culture. As a booth renter, there are risks; going on vacation means still paying rent for your workspace while you are away. Booth renters have no paid time off, health insurance, or retirement benefits. Job Security? Oh yeah, you are only as good to the shop as your consistency with the rent…. If you slip up and string together three weeks of missing those payments… you're out! Also, the glass ceiling I kept running into as a renter was, I had no room for growth, causing me to leave shops after building up clients there. Many shops with this model don't offer many career upgrades like management. The only option for more income is to raise prices, increase volume or offer new services or products.

Commission

In this model, the Barbers and the shop split the revenue based on an agreement between both parties. Commission shops typically pay based on performance and track sales of services. Some shops offer hourly wages in addition to the commission. There's an opportunity to earn more money than in a salaried position, depending on your sales ability. The more services you provide increases, the more commission you earn, which can incentivize you to go harder and convert the shop's customers into clients. In the commission shop, there is more incentive for the management or owner to drive sales and train the staff seeing that the split the shop receives handles operating expenses. Some shops in this model cover the cost of supplies, marketing, cleaning and team building activities. Team building includes trade shows, conventions, meetings, and birthday celebrations. Commission shops are able to provide more for the barbers and invest in the shop overall. As a barber, this may be advantageous while building up your clientele since you won't be liable for a hefty booth rental fee every week. As a commission barber, quality control is important for you to retain customers and uphold the reputation of the shop. These shops thrive off the ability to attract walk-ins.

Split decision

Some people are scared of making more money, while others are scared to let it go. A barber feeling himself and paying a cheap booth rent might look at a commission barber like they're crazy for the percentage they contribute, and vice versa. Before making a decision on what type of shop works, you'll have to first know what you deserve, what you are actually worth, and what you're able to negotiate. There will be barbers that don't wanna pay rent or commissions and they can stay in the rehab and shelters. There will also be barbers that will never raise their service price and stay stuck doing the same cheap people, never leveling up. If you don't have an understanding of economics, confidence, and work ethic, it doesn't matter which shop you choose. Going after the low booth rent may entail a not-so-great location. Choosing the best opportunity with continual learning, guaranteed income, and birthday cake might mean taking a commission split and relying on tips. It's really about what you want, what you can handle and what you have to offer.

Tale of the taper

Starting out as a barber in a shop was a straightforward business model for me. I paid Get Faded $50 a week, and I paid it weekly until I could handle more, rent maxed out at $100. Last century I began working in a booth rent shop, and the cost was usually the equivalent of one or two heads per day. If I adjust those rates for inflation, it would be approximately $300 a week today. Not bad to plug up clippers, get busy and gain exposure.

When I opened my own barbershop, Fade in Full, I wasn't experienced in collecting rent and pricing the cost of booths. We had three chairs in total, and I used one, which left two chairs charging $100 per week. This amount was only guaranteed if the guys were busy. As we grew, we added more chairs, raised rents accordingly, and collected cash until we got a POS system for our card transactions. We only had one system for the entire shop, so I had them do their card transactions on the machine and keep the receipts until the end of the week. If the amount they had in receipts was over the booth rent, I would pay them out of pocket from what I made cutting my clients. I even paid for replacing the receipt paper out of my own pocket. In the early years of Fade in Full, it felt like I bought a job. The upfront expenses for the business and upgrades were all on me, leaving little left for the shop to support itself off booth rent.

During our forced shutdown due to COVID-19, I didn't charge booth rent, unlike some other shops. When we reopened, things started to get challenging. Our new neighbor in the next door space was a bakery that ran ovens nonstop, which caused a lot of heat and discomfort for our clients and barbers. I'm surprised the paint didn't melt off the walls! We had two new hires after the shutdown, and I didn't feel comfortable raising rents on new and seasoned barbers during a slow period. Eventually, the complaints and absences of some of the barbers made me switch to a commission-based model, which turned out to be one of the best decisions I ever made.

If you are an owner, it's crucial to allow the shop to support itself. The staff should not expect you to cut hair all the time, as that is not the reason you opened the shop. The profit margin from booth rent or commission should be enough to free you from depending on cutting hair. Also, your staff can thrive in your absence, assuming they are skilled and competent. As the owner, you should focus on running the business and handling administrative tasks.

In my experience, barbers who complained about booth rent and didn't respect my authority as the owner never fared well.

They didn't respect themselves for squandering away a career opportunity to save a few dollars. As an owner, it's important to charge enough to cover expenses and make a profit. When I was a barber, I always had the demand and numbers, but as an owner, I had to think beyond just cutting hair. As an owner, I learned to choose what's best for the business and to get a return on my invested capital.

Owning and managing a barbershop takes hard work, dedication, and attention to detail. It's essential to charge enough to cover expenses and make a profit, prioritize the business's needs over individual barbers' desires, and stay focused on administrative tasks and running the business effectively. An owner deserves to be compensated for the business risks and the opportunity they provide.

Commission Pros
-Possible higher earnings earning a percentage of all sales
-Possible benefits, PTO, Health Insurance, and Retirement Plan based on shops business model
-Marketing & Advertising that increases customer frequency

Commission Cons
-Shop may require a sales minimum to keep favorable percentage split
-Competition amongst barbers trying to earn incentives
-May have to split tips
-May have to pay commission on retail sales
-Less control over schedule

-Less control over price of service

Booth Rent Pros

-Freedom to control schedule

-Keep all earnings and pay a flat fee for space

-Control over your own marketing

-Control over building your client base

-Set your own price

-Keep earnings from selling your own products

Booth Rent Cons

-Responsibility for all operating expenses

-Providing your own equipment, chairs, products, etc

-No guaranteed income

-Lack of support from shop in building clients & marketing

-No benefits

-Paying rent even when you don't work

Actionable Questions and Steps

Questions

How does the booth rental model influence the overall culture of a barbershop?

- What are the benefits and drawbacks of other business models like commission, hybrid, or franchise for a barbershop?

Action steps

- Assess your business model. If you own a barbershop, is it serving your needs and the needs of your employees? Consider

alternative models.
- Conduct a SWOT analysis of your current business model.

Questions
- Why is professional behavior and personal hygiene important in the barbershop industry?
- How can conflicts in the workplace be effectively resolved?

Action steps
- Reflect on your personal conduct in the workplace. Is there room for improvement?
- Make a commitment to maintaining professional behavior and personal hygiene.

Questions
- How does pricing affect the perception of your service?
- How can a barber balance between offering competitive prices and ensuring profits?

Action steps
- Evaluate your pricing strategy. Are you pricing your services correctly, taking into account your costs, time, and the quality of service?
- Experiment with value-based pricing. Can you offer premium services for a higher price?

- Question: Why is understanding a client's preferences crucial in building a positive barber-client relationship?

- Action step: Practice active listening with each client to fully understand their needs and preferences.

- Question: How does maintaining personal hygiene influence the client's perception of a barber and the barbershop?
- Action step: Develop a routine for personal cleanliness before, during, and after each appointment.

- Question: What effect does punctuality have on client satisfaction and the business flow of the barbershop?
- Action step: Create a schedule that allows you ample time between appointments to prevent delays.

NOTES

WEAPONS OF MASS PRODUCTION

Over the years, my repertoire has changed. In the beginning, I kept two of every pair of each clipper because they used to get hot fast. The evolution of clippers has freed us from having to use oven mitts to hold trimmers and pulling around tangled cords for every cut. My initial set up in the shop was: Two pairs of Andis Master adjustable clippers for my fades, two pairs of Oster Seventy-Six Clippers with detachable blades for my takedowns and two pairs of Andis T-outliners that were zero-gapped for line ups. For my Osters, I usually kept blades OA up to the two blades. For my super old school barbers, one of my cheat codes for wave cuts was the 18-blade. I believe they have discontinued it. It was a blade that was between the 1.5 and the one with pointy shark-like teeth. For decades I used the red Speed-O-Guides for my Andis Masters and was notorious for cutting with broken teeth on those guards.

Today, my current arsenal consists of one pair of Babyliss Gold FX adjustable, one pair of Wireless Oster Fast Feeds, one pair of Wahl Magic Clips, an Andis Close Shaver and two shears I use frequently: one for thinning and one regular. My Babyliss FX handles my bulk and getting bald lines out, My Fast Feeds is what I use for fades, I use my Magic Clips whenever I feel the need to and my Babyliss FX Trimmers have been reliable for balding and lines since day one with the same blade.

What you decide to use for cuts is your discretion. I've tried many different clippers and shears before deciding to stick with what I use. I'm not the guy to nerd out over the specifics of blade lengths and how my clippers were manufactured. At one point, I was interested in customizations and adjustments. Now I prefer to use my clippers fresh out of the box with factory settings. This is a barber book, so we should go over the tools needed to get started.

Clippers:

Clippers are electric hair cutting tools that are essential for creating various hairstyles. They come with different attachments or guards to achieve different hair lengths and textures. Clippers are used to cut and blend hair, create fades, and perform precise and efficient haircuts.

Options:
- Wahl Professional Magic Clip
- Andis Master Cordless Clipper

- Oster Classic 76 Clipper
- BabylissPro Barberology MetalFX Series Clipper
- Andis Fade Master Clipper
- Wahl Professional 5-Star Senior Clipper
- BabylissPro Barberology GoldFX Clipper
- Oster Fast Feed Adjustable Pivot Motor Clipper
- Wahl Professional 5-Star Magic Clip Cordless Clipper
- Andis Professional Ceramic Hair Clipper

Trimmers:

Trimmers, also known as edgers or outline trimmers, are small electric tools primarily used for detailing and shaping hairlines, beards, and mustaches. They are ideal for creating clean and sharp lines and refining the edges of a haircut or beard.

Options:
- Wahl Professional 5-Star Detailer Trimmer
- Andis Professional T-Outliner Trimmer
- BabylissPro Barberology GoldFX Trimmer
- Andis SlimLine Pro Li Trimmer
- Wahl Professional Hero Trimmer
- Oster Fast Feed Adjustable Pivot Motor Trimmer
- Andis GTX T-Outliner Trimmer
- Wahl Professional 5-Star Razor Edger Trimmer
- BabylissPro Barberology RoseFX Trimmer
- Andis Professional Cordless T-Outliner LITrimmer

Shears:

Shears, or barber scissors, are hand-held cutting tools with two sharp blades used for cutting and styling hair. They come in various lengths and designs to accommodate different cutting techniques. Shears are used for precision cutting, texturizing, and creating layers or specific haircut styles.

Options:
- Hattori Hanzo Shears
- Kamisori Shears
- Kasho Shears
- Joewell Shears
- Mizutani Shears
- Jaguar Shears
- Ichiro Shears
- Matsui Shears
- Yasaka Shears
- Bonika Shears

Disinfectants:

Disinfectants are products used to kill or inhibit the growth of bacteria, viruses, and fungi on barbering tools and surfaces. They are crucial for maintaining proper hygiene and preventing the spread of infections in a barbershop. Disinfectants are used to sanitize clippers, trimmers, shears, combs, and other tools between clients.

Options

- Barbicide Disinfectant Solution
- Andis Cool Care Plus
- Wahl Professional Premium Black Cutting Guides Disinfectant Spray
- Oster Spray Disinfectant
- BabylissPro Barberology Clippercide Spray
- Clippercide 5-in-1 Spray
- Mar-V-Cide Clipper Cleaner and Disinfectant
- BlueCo Brands Barbicide Wipes
- MD Barber Equipment Disinfectant Spray
- Equinox International Professional Barber Disinfectant Jar

Aftershaves:

Aftershaves are lotions or balms applied to the skin after a shave to soothe and moisturize. They often contain ingredients like witch hazel, menthol, and essential oils that provide a refreshing and cooling effect. Aftershaves help calm the skin, close pores, and prevent irritation or razor burn, leaving a pleasant scent.

Options
- Clubman Pinaud Classic Aftershave
- Lucky Tiger After Shave and Face Tonic
- Proraso Aftershave Lotion
- Captain's Choice Original Bay Rum Aftershave
- The Art of Shaving After-Shave Balm
- Baxter of California After Shave Balm
- Taylor of Old Bond Street Sandalwood Aftershave

- Nivea Men Sensitive Post Shave Balm
- Floïd Vigoroso Aftershave
- American Crew Post-Shave Cooling Lotion

Each of these plays a role in different aspects of your service, ensuring precision, cleanliness, and client satisfaction. These tools and products deliver high-quality cuts, grooming, and styling services while maintaining hygiene and customer comfort. You can catch them all like Pokémon if you want, however one or two of each should do.

SALONS VS BARBERSHOPS

A Verzuz battle between Salons and Barbershops may end in a tie. People get us confused and although we're different, in some ways, we're similar. Amanda Harris, owner of La Lluvia Beauty and I have talked at length about this. Amanda's insights from her time in Barbershops and Salons shed light on the subtle yet significant differences between both sides. "A salon can be commissioned or rented, and a barbershop can be commissioned or rented. So, in terms of ownership, there isn't much difference between the two," she says. "While there are similarities, such as providing hair services, the main difference lies in the dominant clientele. Most barbershops are male-dominated, while salons tend to have a predominantly female clientele."

"Barbers primarily offer a single type of service that can be completed in a relatively short time, usually between 30 minutes to an hour. This simplicity makes it easier for barbers to calculate their earnings. On the other hand, stylists in salons often engage in various services that can take several hours, making it more challenging to track income accurately." Looking at salons from a barber's view, it would seem like they're killing it over there with clocking in upwards of $600 for one service! "As a stylist, I have to price my services based on estimated labor time, accounting for taxes, product costs, and overhead expenses. It involves more complex calculations compared to barbers, who can easily determine their earnings based on time slots." As barbers, we typically only do one or two people an hour, maybe three or four if you're really fast. With two cuts every hour at a fair price, barbers can make a decent income. We, as barbers, typically don't charge for products depending on what we're using. An enhancements like hair fibers or dye, yes. A few sprays of oil sheen or some astringent? Probably not.

She says, "I price my services by the hour, but I don't always communicate that to clients because it may give the impression that I intentionally take longer to make more money. In reality, I want to accommodate as many clients as possible, maximizing both their satisfaction and my income. Quantity matters." I wasn't expecting her to take this route; apparently, she has the energy for a large quantity throughout the day, whereas I would have to do way more people to match her earnings for a day's work.

"When it comes to maximizing earnings, I prefer shorter appointments with multiple clients rather than spending the entire day with one person. By offering shorter services, I can see more clients and charge them a lower price. It benefits both parties as they pay less while I earn more overall."

"Barbers have an advantage in pricing because they can charge a higher amount for a haircut that takes around 30 minutes to an hour. For example, charging $50-$80 for a quality cut with additional grooming services. This straightforward pricing model simplifies their income calculations."

"Salons often face internal competition and insecurity among stylists. In my experience, some stylists and salon owners limit the growth of others by confining them to specific services or styles. This stifles creativity and inhibits individual progress."

"Barbershops, on the other hand, tend to foster a more cooperative environment. The absence of direct competition among barbers allows them to focus on their work and provide quality service without feeling threatened by their colleagues."

"In my journey through different salons, I encountered situations where communication was lacking or driven by underlying tensions. This made collaboration difficult, hindering the overall salon experience. However, I've also had positive relationships with female stylists who share my transparency and supportive approach."

"Starting a career in the beauty industry can be challenging, especially for fresh graduates. It often requires starting from the bottom, even with prior experience. New stylists must be prepared to humble themselves, work through slower periods, and build trust with clients gradually."

"Patience is crucial for new stylists. It takes time to establish trust and build a solid client base. Impatience can lead to prematurely giving up or missing out on opportunities to showcase one's skills and gain referrals."

Amanda went deep into the nuances of the salon and barbershop industry. Her experiences highlight the differences in clientele, service offerings, pricing models, and the importance of fostering supportive and transparent environments within these establishments. Understanding these distinctions is essential for both professionals and clients seeking the best fit for their hairstyling needs.

WHAT THEY REALLY WANT FROM A BUYER

**"BUYERS do business with you, not with your company
and not with your technology."**
- Joanne Black

Sell Yourself

Selling yourself as a barber is essential for growing your clients and building a successful business book. To be successful, you need to be able to communicate your value to customers to convert them into clients and show them why they should choose you over other barbers in the area.

When you sell yourself as a barber, one important thing to remember is your unique selling proposition (USP). This is what sets you apart from other barbers. For example, you may have a certain type of cutting technique or network of contacts that sets you apart or a specific niche you specialize in. Whatever your USP is, it should be highlighted in your marketing materials and communicated to potential clients or shops searching for free agents. This entails knowing your strengths and weaknesses. Don't be delusional. If you know you're not good with time, do not lead with that or bother with appointments.

Another important aspect of selling yourself as a barber is your appearance and attitude. Your appearance should be professional, fresh and clean at all times. This will show potential clients you take pride in your work, care about your own appearance and are dedicated to your craft. Additionally, your attitude should be friendly, approachable, and welcoming. This will put potential clients at ease and make them feel more comfortable entrusting you with their hair.

In addition to your USP and appearance, another way to sell yourself as a barber is through building relationships with your clients. By making an effort to get to know your clients, you will be able to build trust and loyalty that way. This will make them more likely to return to your shop and recommend you to other people in their network.

You can use traditional and online marketing methods to market yourself as a Barber. You can create a website using Wix or Squarespace. You can create social media accounts on apps like Linkedin, Instagram and Facebook. A business listing on Google with contact info, pictures and reviews is a great lead generation tool. I'd suggest getting a QR code on your cards or on your mirror that can link your clients straight to your review page.

You can also use flyers, brochures, and business cards to market your services. Create a portfolio of your work and showcase it on your website and social media accounts. Instagram reels, Youtube Shorts, and TikTok videos are a great way to show your personality with your short form content. These types of videos tend to attract a younger crowd. Our young Barber Lex has been really good at making videos like this. She takes funny jokes about the shop and acts them out on camera with improv videos. The more relatable or comedic your videos are, the more people will engage and share your content. This will give potential clients a sense of your skills, style and personality.

The key to selling yourself as a barber is to clearly communicate your value, maintain a professional appearance and attitude, build relationships with your clients, and market yourself effectively. As a barber, you'll have to understand the fundamentals of sales and marketing in addition to your skills to grow your client base and build a successful business.

If you had a fresh start with all of your clippers and skill set and needed a shop to work in, which one of these do you choose?
A) A high-volume, low-price haircut shop
B) A low-volume, high-price shop

Some choose A for the guaranteed flow of people, while others choose B, attracted to receiving a higher price. Now if you asked me today, I'm choosing B, and here's why: I prefer delayed gratification. Going to a shop with low volume puts the ball in my court to garner attention. I actually have to go in there and earn my clients with exceptional customer experience. Higher price points will weed out unreliable customers and tire kickers. Higher prices often indicate a higher quality shop environment where barbers and customers are comfortable. There is value in the barber you can become if you choose a situation where you're forced to step your game up with service and sales. Now I know what you're thinking. What if I'm just starting out and wanna do as many cuts as possible? Ok, then maybe A works for the barber who wants to practice. You have some perks with A because you work on speed and consistency. There's no right or wrong answer. Either way, you have to learn how to convert those customers to clients, and to do that, you need to be able to influence and persuade. That is the essence of sales.

Selling is life

You've been selling and persuading others since birth, using charm, charisma, and innocence to get what you want, like extra sprinkles on your ice cream sundae. You've mastered the art of getting people to give you what you want. In this profession, you offer value once you have proven yourself to the marketplace. A barber in the early stages is like a baby needing a pacifier to crawl and explore a new world. A Barber with moderate skill is a teenager, ready for more responsibility but still needs guidance. A senior Barber might feel like a partner in a tired marriage in need of a spark. All types have a myriad of challenges that call for the same solution — knowing "How To Sell." With sales, you have to have what your prospect wants and needs. Selling to them is important, but selling for them is even more important.

Let's begin with the most fundamental case study. You've made the leap of putting all your eggs in one basket, have your arsenal of tools, need to cut, and don't know where to begin.

Sales should be about bringing value to people, not extracting it from them. You need to have something people need or want before you can sell anything. Qualifying leads means filtering through the rush and focusing on the best clients that fit your criteria. Let's take a moment to acknowledge the types of clients that may not be the best fit for your business.

Clients who are consistently broke, late, last-minute callers, non-tippers, dirty, fidgety, and constantly switching barbers aren't the best for you.

Most Barbers have cookie-cutter answers for the type of clients they want to serve. No matter who you want you're going to attract people from your lifestyle regardless. You may have lower standards while you're still learning. Once you're well known and in demand, you reserve the right to cut whoever doesn't fit your requirements. Narrowing down the pool of potential customers to the most desirable people is where you need sales skills to separate yourself from the pack. You gotta close those folks and earn your chance to convert them from customer to client.

Types of Customers

1. **Bargain hunters** - They only care about getting the best quality for the lowest price. Some of these people don't really care about hair unless they have something super important going on. They may even try to cut their own hair, go to an inexperienced barber, or run a great barber into the ground who hasn't realized their marketplace value yet. Dealing with these types may cause you to have to fire a client, demand what you deserve, or possibly do a cut if you're practicing or just bored.

2. **Frequent Flier-** These are the type of people who needs to be serviced once or sometimes twice a week. These types can be problematic if they aren't willing to pay the price of frequent service. They may consider a touch-up or a freshen-up for a discounted haircut. Also prone to pushbacks and other issues from changing styles often. They're great if you're efficient with time and money. The cool thing about these types is you don't have to do much work. Since they are frequent, you are basically touching up your own work. You don't have to go above & beyond every time unless they are changing styles often.

3. **Indecisive-** Never knows what they want. If they trust your judgment, they're worth your time. If not, they will eat up your time with consultation, look in the mirror every chance they get, and even walk back up to you to fix something while you're working on your next client. They are a nightmare if you aren't highly skilled

at cutting and dealing with people. Dealing with these types, you should be able to look at someone and know what looks good on them. Make suggestions, minimize the options and agree on the style before you begin. DO NOT let them say, "Let's try it, and if I don't like it, we can do it another way" Because that can turn into two or three haircuts during one appointment. If you have time and they are willing to pay for more than one haircut, then go for it.

4. **Never Satisfied-** Also can be a nightmare. They already have a problem you can't fix. Maybe receding hairline, low self-esteem, or underlying appearance situation. Beware of these types; they will expect you to work a miracle on them. Here is where you have to be somewhat of a therapist. A confidence booster, so to speak. If you are able to blend in an insecurity like hair loss or do a performance enhancing style, you may be able to satisfy them. I've literally had like five or six clients who were dealing with the same issues of hair loss, and I was saving them every week by caring for their hair in a way that preserved what they had as opposed to the Barbers that were rushing and cutting them without noticing the light spots and growth patterns.

5. **Big Tipper-** They are incredible if they tip well and value you. Some will expect that because they tip well, they can skip the line, catch a free one, or rollover tips into another service. Tips are only tips and are appreciated as such. Doesn't always uncover new privileges. Tipping

consistently over the years gives more room for benefits than just for a few cuts. Use your discretion when dealing with a big tipper.

6. **Raging Narcissist-** This type will expect you to drop everything for their hair. They demand all of your attention even when it isn't their time yet. They will attempt to guilt you at every price increase, mention of vacation, or unavailability. Beware of people who force you to have to deny them and swear it's your fault, as if you owe them when you are simply doing your job or living your life. They don't own you. Keep in mind that you have a life and other responsibilities besides being available for haircuts. Draw the line and never let people take advantage of you for money. Once you're in demand, you can replace a client and life goes on.

7. **Chair/Shop Hopper-** They will go to whoever is available, popular, or convenient. Don't become attached to these types. You're expendable to them, and both of your lives go on with or without each other. There's no converting them into a client. They are extra money if you have time.

8. **Tea sippers-** They have all the gossip about everything. Other shops, Barbers, and current events. If they come to you shitting on another barber, most likely they're saying the same about you when they go everywhere else. These may be the WORST. Although the shop is a place where people talk, you want to have it as drama free as possible. This type may not care who they offend and

can cause tension in a place where people should be able to relax. My way of dealing with this may not be yours. If it becomes too offensive, I stop the convo. Usually, if they are saying something bad about someone, I respond with something good about them. Also, you don't want a reputation for talking greasy about people because when the streets say, "they said," you are automatically a part of 'they'. We're adults, and we don't need to be playing the telephone game.

9. **Hard worker-** A great customer or client because you know they will always have consistent income and need service to maintain a quality of life. The flipside here is that they'll need to be able to grow with you if you have to increase your prices. When they get a raise, that should mean you get one too. Also, remember they will be one of the first to request you work around their work schedule which can be taxing on your time if they have a crazy shift or do overtime. If you become close with them and they take care of you for taking care of them, this is a good client to have.

10. **Lifetime value-** We all want people who will support us no matter what. These are the ones who pay the bills. Lifetime value can come in the form of who has grossed the most over time, adds to the vibe of the shop, brought in referrals, and been around the most time.

11. **Influencer-** Every group has a leader. You can often end up working for a whole friend group, staff, or team if you cut the person who has the most influence over everyone.

This person will bring you the most people. It's tough to identify these types unless they arrive with the group. However, if you attend networking events or want to target a specific group, you want to close in on the main decision-maker to catch everyone else as well.

Identifying these qualities in people will come easy over time. At times some will be a mix of a few or all of one. You decide which types of customers work best for you, your shop, or the stage of your career you're currently in. Who you attract depends on what type of Barber you are.

Before opening Fade in Full, I had a large clientele. Most were referrals and die-hard fans because I was affordable and available. Barbers will start immediately thinking that the cheat code for instant success is being cheap and available. I had a hard time saying no initially, so I didn't have much free time. I was the only person people trusted with their hair in the early Fade in Full days. I hated those Saturdays when I'd be swamped with a full day of appointments, both phones ringing, and people would STILL pull up, walk in and ask me, "How many heads you got?" It was insane!!! I can't make this up! It's still befuddling to think back on some of the ways people made it difficult to do business with me. They'd wait last minute, call my cell phone on Saturday afternoon and get no answer. Then call the shop phone just for Mr Wes to tell them I was cutting somebody. Then hours later, that same person would pull up and walk in while I was still cutting somebody else in the evening!!! I'd refer them to Mr Wes or suggest a better day and time just to get rejected. They would get upset and walk out and do this all over again next Saturday. Being a good barber doesn't make you a great salesman. I'll be honest, I didn't do much prep or planning on how I would sell my barbers or my shop to everyone before we opened up. I figured that since I could cut very well, I could grab some mirrors and chairs and have a shop!!! Not quite, I learned from the Wolf of Wall Street, Jordan Belfort, that in order to close on a sale, your prospect has to have a high level of certainty in these three things. Your product/service, your company, and you! Early in the game, we were scoring low in some areas. Even if people were sold on me, that's ALL they were sold on; my service to them. Not my co-sign of another barber or ability to grow talent. Not the vibe or culture either. They were only certain about a haircut from me. Dealing with those early objections gave us tough skin and grit to handle it. In sales, people will say no. Eventually, the no's will lead to a yes. Those nos in the beginning also turned Mr Wes into a KILLER! He spent time in the shop, learning, listening, and watching. Seeing him there all the time made some people give him a chance to cut their hair. After a year, he was telling people NO because he had built up his own following, and his schedule became full. I take great pride in seeing him making good money. Being able to move at his own pace and purchase a home now is a blessing. It's all possible because he was there to go through the building process and remembers how hectic things were.

Is sales an important aspect for barbers? Besides getting a customer for the first time, when do you have to sell? Maybe you have a product or an extra service. Maybe you have a shop that you want to be a part of. Maybe you want to open a shop and have to make a lasting impression on a landlord or group for commercial space. Whatever the case may be, you have to know the desired outcome for your prospect and for you!

As an aspiring barber, learning about sales is crucial to success. Offering a haircut to a new client, hiring a new team member, seeking investment, your ability to effectively sell your skills, services, and vision can make all the difference. At the heart of sales is the concept of providing value to others. When selling a haircut, this means ensuring your clients understand the quality and care that goes into every cut you give. It means highlighting the unique skills and experience you bring to the table and making sure your clients know they'll be getting a great haircut they'll love. Early in the game, it may feel weird to brag about how good you're giving it up. As long as you stand firm on what your strengths are, you remain true to the game.

When you're selling the opportunity of a job or key role, it's about creating a work culture and atmosphere that's fulfilling and rewarding for everyone. This means highlighting the competitive pay and benefits you offer, as well as the opportunities for growth and development within your team and shop. If you're selling equity, it's about providing an opportunity for investors to participate in the growth and success of your business. This means being able to articulate your vision for the future clearly, and demonstrate how your investment can help you achieve that vision. Within your vision has to be a clear path on how an investor receives a return on capital. Don't run off on the plug! Maintaining a reputation for making money increases your opportunity to make more money. Successful sales is understanding what your clients and prospects want and need, and being able to communicate how you can meet those needs clearly. You can thrive in business and achieve your dreams with the right approach and mindset.

As a barber, one of your greatest assets is your ability to build relationships with your clients. It's easy to get caught up in using Customer Relationship Manager (CRM) tools and technology, but don't forget the importance of personal connections. A CRM is a tech database that we use to interact with customers and potential clients. We were using LeadOwl. Many successful barbers and salespeople have a knack for connecting with people and understanding their needs. Remember, when it comes to sales, it's not just about the money. There are countless other barbers and shops out there offering similar services. So for you to truly stand out, you have to understand what your clients are looking for and offer them real value.

Marketing vs. Sales

Many people confuse sales and marketing, but they're different concepts. Marketing is all about creating interest and awareness for customers, while sales are focused on getting customers to make a purchase. I spent two years managing the marketing for our barbershop with some success, but I wouldn't consider

71

myself an expert. I focused more on creating engaging content than the technical aspects of running online ads.

As we approached July 2021, we realized our marketing strategy needed a refresh. We had attracted a lot of interest in me as an individual, but not necessarily in the shop. To boost our walk-in traffic and keep cash flowing, we decided to bring in a marketing specialist who specializes in barbershops and salons. We found a guy named Mike from Toronto who was skilled in running social media ads and had a unique perspective on what types of pictures to post and how to write ad copy.

Mike proposed a strategy of raising our prices, increasing operating time, and running a 30% off campaign for new customers. He also created a funnel where prospects could click an ad online, enter their information in a CRM, and receive a call from one of our staff members to close the sale. As the shop owner, I was responsible for making these calls. At first, it was challenging. Some people were rude or uninterested, but I learned quickly and developed a framework for the calls. I found the best time to call, the best questions to ask, and the right information to provide, all while keeping the calls under 10 minutes. This campaign lead the shop to its best year of gross revenue, a record-breaking month, and a consistent flow of new clients. The experience taught me valuable lessons about sales and marketing, and I believe Mike's strategy was a key factor in our success.

At our barbershop, we use a strategy of identifying leads as hot, warm, or cold. A hot lead is a customer ready to book an appointment or is already a client. A warm lead is someone who has visited our shop before but is not a full-time client. A cold lead is someone who's uninterested, has no prior knowledge of our shop, or had a negative experience with us.

When making a courtesy call, it's important to mention that it's a courtesy call and when the offer expires. During the call, we also make a note of any specific needs or concerns the prospect may have, such as looking for a new barber or wanting to try a better barbershop.

Prospects often have questions about our location, prices, services offered, and hours of operation. We make sure to have answers to frequently asked questions, such as if we cut children's hair or if we're open late. Additionally, we can handle objections that may arise during the call, such as a prospect claiming their current barber charges less or they had a negative experience at our shop before.

To close the call and book a customer, we simply lead them to schedule an appointment. We ensure the customer is satisfied with their experience and are confident in the services we provide.

Example of Call Script on Last Page

Follow up
You need notes to follow up. If they mention what they get, who they know, or when they're available, add this info to notes for

yourself or whoever follows up on the call. Intelligence gathering is key on the initial call to set up a follow-up. Try to set up a date to follow up. For someone who is interested, ask them when it is best to check back in. For someone not interested, I suggest hitting them back like six months later or whenever it's dead-ass slow for you. If you call back months later and remember something you discussed, you might land one. I know you're probably thinking like this is a lot to go through for a haircut. It's not just about one cut though. It's about you building up clients, people who may be religiously spending money with you every week. Building a rapport or meaningful relationship with people makes them want to see you more often. Even if you don't become their main barber, they may remember you if their guy isn't available. Before technology, we used to be able to do this with memory leading to people always recognizing us as barbers when they saw us. To be a full time barber, it has to be synonymous with your identity so you are top of mind anytime someone is looking for a haircut.

Inbound calls
How to answer the phone

Thank you for calling (Name of shop). My name is (your name). How can I help? Or Assist?... simple...

Gather intel by using questions from the aforementioned need-to-know list.

Listen more than you speak unless they take the subject too far away from haircuts and the Barbershop. We don't want to waste time on the phone. We can talk about whatever they want once they're in the Barber Chair.

Name of Customer/Client
What type of Service do they want
Their Availability
If they want a certain person to serve them

How to close After a Cut.

You want three things after a haircut: rebooking, referrals, and reviews. Also gratuity, which we don't talk about enough.

Here are some ways to gain more tips.

1. Smile.

When you smile, you're more inviting to have a conversation with. I've seen many people walk into shops and sit down without saying anything. If they are making eye contact, a smile can be an ice breaker or a mood booster. Break the tension and feel good about serving a client or meeting a new person.

2. Finding something you and your client have in common.

In order to find out what you like, one person has to be an active listener while the other person is talking. Let the conversation flow like a game of catch where the person holding the ball is the one speaking. Keep it casual; it doesn't have to be 21 questions or a script. A talk about a common interest can make the service fly by fast and leave your client inspired, satisfied, and knowing that they have a barber they can identify with.

3. Make a suggestion based on client needs.

If you were paying attention during number two, this should be pretty easy. Suggestions shouldn't be limited to just hair. However, in order to maintain professionalism, if they confide to you about family, friends, or children, use an example of what you have already experienced. Speak about your end result or lesson you learned without making a clear suggestion. Leave the personal decisions for your client to decide. If you tell them to break up with their cheating baby mama and they end up on child support, you will be the blame.

4. Ensure great service by getting a clear understanding of what the client is looking for.

A lot of barbers skip this and just do whatever they want. If you have a client from a different city or region, they may explain the cut in a way that you misunderstood. If you aren't sure, ask if they have a picture of themselves with the cut they want. If that doesn't work, pull out Google, and search for what they want. A picture is worth a 1000 words and in this case, a tip.

5. Let them know how much you appreciate the opportunity to serve them.

Sales Culture

Our shop has been on a commission-based model since the rough and dark times of 2020. We went into a new location which doubled our operating expenses while still charging a booth rent fee. The booth rent wasn't enough to cover the cost of doing business, and the barbers at the time were complaining about how much the rent was. Funny how some were complaining while watching Netflix and scrolling Instagram; two non-income-producing activities. Our customer flow was slowed down due to fear of covid, and the regulations only allowed a certain capacity in the shop. All of these setbacks pushed me to make the decision to switch our shop to a commission model. Before this time, I had no experience in a commission shop. We split the revenue on every service, and there were no complaints about rents because you contribute based on your performance and quantity. Little did I know I was introducing a sales culture to our barbershop. The ball was in my court to feed the shop leads and also to show the newbies how to retain those leads. In the beginning, I ran ads nonstop. I put people in front of the blue wall at our shop, and we created content so the world could get to know more about the barbers, their personalities, and the culture of the shop. We did tip Tuesday videos with hair suggestions, highly opinionated top 5 rapper videos, and sports prediction videos. The inspiration behind this was creating content to attract like-minded people to relatively unknown barbers. Sports and music are easy topics to debate, and we received way more comments and walk-ins from our esoteric views on rap and sports. It felt like a marketing genius. Once we started to gain some momentum, I was able to see the numbers. The numbers mattered because everyone needed to reach a quota to keep the lights on and make a living. At first, I only shared the numbers with people one-on-one, and if someone started slipping, it was a conversation. If someone did well, then also a one-on-one congratulations. There were a few people in the shop who were always in the middle of the pack. Didn't really go up or down in productivity. With nobody knowing what others were doing, it allowed people to slip under the radar. So I decided to up the stakes and share the numbers so we could really see what was up with everybody. It took a week or two to gather all of the stats. I knew the quantity that everyone was doing but not the individual records. Like best day, best month, best week, or even best year. I had to do this for the team manually. Once I gathered the stats, I called a meeting and brought in a big whiteboard with the main records on it. The stats were color coated with red, meaning someone was on the decline, and green, meaning someone was on the rise. Black just meant they were steady. With that meeting, everything changed, and we did our first contest. The first contest wasn't directly related to the numbers on the board though. It was a "who gets the most reviews in a month" contest which was a brilliant idea I credit to CDB, who eventually became the winner of that contest and won some Beats headphones. The contest was a win for the shop overall because it achieved something I'd always wanted for the shop, and that was for us to rank higher and have more visibility on Google. Everyone went hard during that contest, and it allowed people to shine and push for reviews with their names mentioned.

We went on to have a record-breaking month shortly after that. That was kinda like a tester for the real true sales-related challenge. After all of my data analytics, I realized nobody ever did 50 services in a week since we've been recording stats. I was pretty sure it's been done before, but since we used to be on booth rent, there was no record of it or reason to record what everyone was doing. So I went to the Game Stop, grabbed an Oculus virtual game system, and announced our "first to 50'. Everyone had a month to achieve this. This contest was a lot more competitive. I'll be honest there were a few who didn't try to win at all, and their lack of effort was exposed. These contests really show who's bought into the team culture and competition and who's just ... there. Anyway, the competitors fought it out to the bloody end. After the two top dogs came close, Pat edged it out with over 50 in the last week of that month. He was the first to hit 50. But looking back at the month, he broke an unintended record of the most ever in one month with close to 200 services!!!! Incredible! He even beat my monthly records. What Pat has done was remarkable because when he started with us, he used to butcher some cuts. He even was on thin ice a few times over some issues. I'm extremely impressed with him for turning everything around in a short time. Holding those two records still to this day and getting out of his own way. Sticking to the grind when things got rough and winning contests. So far, he is the holder of three records within our shop. This would have never been possible if we didn't implement our stats, our leaderboard and give our people more to work towards besides money, and that all happened with sales culture.

Refunds

Millions of dollars are LOST yearly in Barbershops on refunds!

Like most dilemmas in the shop, it should be solved by a three-step process. To handle unhappy customers, first, we try to fix the issue with the cut by working with the current barber to make adjustments. If the problem can't be resolved by the current barber, we bring in a more experienced professional to rectify the cut. If the customer is still not satisfied, we offer a complimentary service from a skilled barber or, as a last resort, a refund or free cut. While it is unfortunate when a customer isn't satisfied, we strive to find a resolution that satisfies the customer and maintains a positive reputation for the shop. I have to stress here that active listening and good communication are key to avoiding having to go through this stuff. Regular training and meetings help keep everyone on point and aligned in giving the customers a good experience.

Extra Credit

Many of your clients own businesses or have side hustles that can gain some exposure through you. A logo on a selfie wall, your shop's fliers, or a brand collaboration can be profitable with a proper sales campaign. Essentially this is B2B, so understanding the goals and needs of your customer comes before offering the features and benefits. First, we need to know if we're able to provide any value to them. A quick call, text, or email is a possible way to explore this revenue stream. Let's begin with the people with whom you have close relationships with first. Collaborating with local businesses can create mutually beneficial partnerships. These partnerships can bring more attention and awareness to both the barbershop and the collaborating business.

For example, partnering with your clients' clothing stores and offering discounts on haircuts for their customers. The clothing store could offer discounts on clothing for customers who get their haircut at the barbershop. Collaborating with other businesses not only brings in fresh clientele but also fosters a mutually beneficial relationship. By partnering, you can leverage each other's customer base and reputation, leading to repeat business and positive word-of-mouth. Get creative and align your collaborations with your barbershop's unique brand and values. For example, our barbershop, Fade in Full, has reached out to educators and community organizations to offer free haircuts at school events and partnered with Black Boys Read Too to promote literacy through book clubs and events held at our shop. Remember, the goal of sales is to serve the community, not just make a profit. Approach each opportunity with integrity and a commitment to doing what's right for your customers.

Actionable Questions

The following questions are to be answered honestly, as this serves as a recap of the main point and a checklist for you.

1. What challenges did the author face in the early days of their barbershop, and how did they handle difficult customers?

2. Why is sales an important aspect for barbers? Can you think of situations where barbers would need to sell besides getting a customer for the first time?

3. What does it mean to provide value to clients as a barber? How can barbers ensure their clients understand the quality and care they put into their work?

4. How does sales differ from marketing? Why did the author decide to bring in a marketing specialist for their barbershop?

5. Can you explain the strategy the author implemented with the marketing specialist, Mike, to boost their business? How did this strategy contribute to their success?

6. What is the significance of identifying leads as hot, warm, or cold? How does it impact the approach when making courtesy calls to potential clients?

7. What are some common questions and objections prospects may
have during a courtesy call? How can barbers address these questions and objections effectively?

8. How do barbers close the call and book a customer? What steps do they take to ensure the customer is satisfied and confident in their services?

9. How important are personal connections and building relationships with clients for barbers? Why is it crucial to go beyond using CRM tools and focus on understanding clients'

needs?

10. How can barbers offer real value to their clients, considering many other barbers and shops are offering similar services?

NOTES

DOLLARS AND SENSE

"To become financially independent, you must turn part of your income into capital; turn capital into enterprise; enterprise into profit; turn profit into investment; and turn investment into financial independence."
—Jim Rohn

Mattress money

Six months were left to serve on my three-year sentence when I discovered Rich Dad Poor Dad at 22 years old. I was carjacked outside of the barbershop, and retaliation resulted in a house fire. I was charged with Attempted Arson at 19 years old and pleaded guilty. Prior to that, my financial literacy was limited to saving for a car or paying bills. Robert Kiyosaki delivered words that read like a five mic classic! I was glued to that book and completed it at record speed. The principles still hold true about the difference between liabilities and assets. Once I was released from prison, I wanted to execute what I had learned and digest anything else

85

written by Rich Dad. Cashflow Quadrant and Retire Young Retire Rich were good books, respectively. Financial momentum slowed abruptly due to my circle of influence. I wasn't reading as much and didn't yet have a credit card or bank account. Just money in the mattress. Cash for everything. My expenses were simple: Barber supplies, booth rent, phone bill, car insurance, car repairs, music production, and leisure. Three years in custody was followed by years of survival mode. Police raids while living with my grandma, and the anxiety of rebuilding a new life. Some of my friends lived carefree, while others were handling parental responsibilities. I was working on plans and writing raps during my free time. Without access to capital, I had to raise money however I could. Barbering and mixtapes put a brown Pontiac Bonneville on the road three months after I was home. Once I was back on my own in 2009, some of those Rich Dad principles started to kick in again. Rent and car repairs were urgent priorities. Liabilities outweighed the assets though. They say the black dollar lasts less than a day in our economy, and that was true for my checking account. No strategy or investment activity yet. I was losing the rat race, selling CDs to the corner stores, buying supplies, paying booth rent, and blowing the rest. My concept of saving was only to make a purchase. No emergency fund, no retirement plan, no real stability. Week to week and month to month like a hamster in the wheel running nowhere fast. Thanks to Rich Dad and reading that book, I knew I couldn't go far living like that.

Knowledge, wisdom & understanding

Bad habits are hard to shake. Conventional wisdom says we should save 10% of our income, invest 20%, live off the rest, and keep our living expenses in an emergency account for six months. Spending less than making more at the time was easier for me. After a few lifestyle changes, the first step was cleaning up my credit. Wiping my debts clean so I could start fresh. I'd been in cash so long, and my outstanding debt was mostly from ambulance rides and unpaid utility bills. It didn't take very long to pay off. I contacted whoever I owed, negotiated an amount, and chipped away at it monthly.

One of my clients, my beloved friend Drew, became a financial advisor, so I opened up an IRA with him. Thirty may be kinda late for some of you to consider retirement, but where I come from, retirement could be a life sentence up top. An IRA is an Investment Retirement Account. I got a Roth IRA, and he explained to me that I pay tax on contributions as opposed to paying the taxes of tomorrow on the withdrawal. Whoever came up with the concept was brilliant. Drew would always suggest getting life insurance, which is a pretty solid wealth-building tool as well. I continued to buy clothes, crash cars, and get scrapped off the floor at bars instead. Drew slowly broadened my limiting beliefs. I always assumed life insurance was about leaving an inheritance and taking care of funeral expenses. If I'd been contributing to a policy, I'd be able to use the life benefit now. So instead of walking into a bank and asking for a loan, I could just take money from my own "bank."

Hindsight is 20/20, so instead of looking back and saying, "If I knew what I know," let's look at today and use what we know now to execute and never go broke again.

Culture & Freedom

At most barber trade shows, our professionals are watching contests, checking out clippers, and trying on the barber jackets. There's a finance class for barbers, and it's usually empty. Barbers always ask for advice about how to make more money, and some demand lower booth rent or a higher commission split. If you refuse to cut the fat of your own personal spending, won't charge a higher price, or plan on investing, then rent and commissions aren't your problem. None of us can work forever. You're a barber, and money will come fast. Instead of wasting it or blowing it, you have the choice to be smart with it. Now is the best time to get your money right. It doesn't matter how much you make; what's important is how much you keep.

Power

Sobriety invited new routines, like going home safe with cash. Since I wasn't out at the parties, I began to read Retire Young Retire Rich by Robert Kiyosaki again. I piled up a few months of living expenses in my savings; at that time, I was paying myself $600 weekly to my checking account and transferring $200 to my savings account. I began investing once I had three months' worth of living expenses in my savings account. One of my clients sent me a link for a free stock on Robinhood. Robinhood is a mobile app used for investing, trading stocks, and crypto. It was easy to navigate after I claimed my free stock, and it became my favorite fintech platform. After trying different strategies, I prefer plain old buy and hold; buying shares in companies I believe in. With a competent CEO, good quarterly earnings, a solid value proposition, and great market share, how can you go wrong investing your funds there? Dollar-cost averaging with the top 5 companies on the market is a great way to start. DCA is a strategy when you contribute that same amount to your portfolio weekly or monthly, no matter what! The market is up? Invest. The market is down? Invest! You should love when it's down because you get good stocks on sale.

Just think… If you found an index fund or individual stock that has an average return of 10% every year, you're beating any savings account out there. $500 monthly contributions potentially become 6k a year, and I didn't factor in gains during the year or do any math on the compound interest from years of dollar cost averaging consistently. $500 is too much right now? Cool, start with whatever you can afford. The days of us having to know a broker or needing large amounts to get in the market are over. It's your easiest shot at ownership without actually being the founder of a company. Invest with a plan to hold no less than five years. Focus on the great companies and take a look at what the hedge funds are investing in. A hedge fund is a limited partnership of private investors whose money is managed by professional fund managers. Don't get shaken up over the news and fear. The news may say it's all over, and if we're still here to talk about it, it ain't over yet. Keep investing. Invest even when fear and doubt are at the highest and buy those low prices. Every time the market has hit an all-time low, it's bounced back over the next 12 months, so don't let the "end of the world" narratives in the media scare you. It's really the end when it's the end.

Chasing highs only works for weed smokers, not investors. Just because an IPO (initial public offering) gets news coverage or an option strategy becomes popular on Wall Street Bets shouldn't be the signal for you to jump in like the rest of the sheep. What goes up fast usually falls fast. I've taken some losses in stocks, so I can speak from experience. Investing with the hopes of getting rich fast almost never happens. If you do hit big off a tip or stroke of good luck, God bless you, do well to take some of your earnings over to an investment that is conservative. There are a bunch of options traders who were all the way up in 2020 that are delivering pizzas now because they didn't know how to handle their money. I look at wealth building as a steady climb. The market goes up and down like a yoyo. Imagine you were playing with that yoyo while walking up the stairs and never stopped. Ten years from now, you will be on top of the steps no matter what's happening with the yoyo. That'll always be the result for you, no matter which asset class you choose, as long as you keep investing.

One of my favorite ways to invest is in collectibles. It's an easy asset class to hop in if you love pop culture or sports. I've been collecting comics forever. The comics are separated by age and appreciated based on the popularity of a character, movie, or TV series. The key issues are the books with a significant event, the first appearance of a character, the last appearance of a character, an autograph or some variant art cover. The CGC books are graded for guaranteed quality assurance and are protected by a plastic case. The grading system is standard, with a higher grade increasing the value of your book. One new trend I've noticed is that copper and modern-age books are increasing in value if the cover has a barcode. The barcode indicates it's been distributed to a newsstand. Since comic stores immediately care for the books with bags and boards, your newsstand edition had touched many hands and sat on a shelf for months before it was purchased. So if you have a good copy of a newsstand, it's more rare. In the collectible game, rare things and exclusivity is king.

Sports cards have experienced a resurgence amongst the NFT (non-fungible token) craze. Buying those cards could serve you better than betting at the casino. No knock on the casino; gambling ain't the same as investing though. Card value appreciates and depreciates based on player performance and career stats. I often hear these long debates about stats, yet the players are making all the bread, and the spectators are just being entertained. I'd have more interest in a Bills Super Bowl run if I owned a few Josh Allen rookie cards. When they win, I'd be live on IG jumping through a flaming table with Bills Mafia and omw cash out a few of those cards before the parade starts. Similar to comic books, cards also have a grading system with PSA. At the time of writing, the highest card ever sold was a 1952 Mickey Mantle for a staggering 12.5 million!

The cryptocurrency and NFT communities have been kinda hush since the gold rush of pandemic times. None of us have ever identified "Satoshi Nakamoto" who is the pseudonym name of the creator of Bitcoin, yet we've bet on BTC at some point. Bitcoin and the alt coins have birthed some millionaires in the pre Metaverse era.

The emergence of crypto came shortly after the housing market crash and recession. A decentralized financial system rose from the shadows of the dark web to hedge against an economy that's been devastated by predatory NINJA (no income, no job, approved) loans, corporate bailouts, and tethered to interest rates by a Federal Reserve Bank. One huge difference between Bitcoin and cash is the limited quantity and a set amount of 21 million BTC distributed over time. Whereas the Federal Reserve prints cash whenever we have a world dilemma that devalues our USD. Since the printer has been running wild, we've received $9 trillion, leading to inflation, universal basic income, and changing world order.

I've known people that hit massive gains investing in crypto and brought them into the shop to teach us the basics. They taught us about cryptocurrency, coin utility, how to obtain coins, investment fundamentals, and more. The process of acquiring coins can be daunting for the moderately computer-literate person. Two-hour Zoom meetings with shared screens, VPNs, gas fees, and a speculative advisor who expects to be compensated may sound intimidating. Whatever hoops you jump through for a coin like Safemoon and Shiba INU are the same hoops you'll have to jump through to withdraw your capital gains. You can buy coins on the investment apps; however, you don't have access to your own wallet to actually use and own the currency. I use the Coinbase wallet, although my advisors suggest getting a ledger. A ledger is like an offline external hard drive that holds the coins for you. Whatever you decide to do, make sure you keep your password and wallet keys in a safe place off the internet or never in your phone notes. The wallet keys are a series of words that give you access to your pot of gold. Hackers have advanced and can steal your precious assets if you aren't smart with storage. Stories in the news have covered investors who have been holding Bitcoin since the early 2010s and have billions waiting for them yet can't claim them because they don't know their keys or have lost their hard drives. Investing in crypto can be fun and exciting; however, you need to proceed with caution. At the time of writing this, the crypto space had experienced a collapse due to the malpractice of one Sam Bankman Fried. His actions with FTX have caused an entire exchange to fall and for billions to vanish in days. He was a 30-year-old CEO and crypto billionaire who created his worth and fooled the likes of reputable hedge fund investors like BlackRock and trusted media outlets like CNBC. More details will be revealed, so there is no need to go too deep right now. I advise you to do your due diligence when it comes to investing in this space. The rewards are great, yet the crypto infrastructure is developing and not yet resistant to human corruption. My losses in crypto come from holding onto some coins way too long and not selling at the right time to pull my gains out. I experienced this with the coins and also from investing in Riot Blockchain, which at the time was the only crypto-related stock on the NYSE. I put some money in Riot in 2017, it went up, and I held on. It trended downward, and I sold some. I kept some shares until they went under a dollar during a crash and sold my last shares out. Months later, crypto was back in the news and I saw Riot still on my watchlist, and it had shot way past the peak of when I had it! If I had just held on and didn't sell at all, my hundreds would've been thousands! I broke a major rule in any business by buying high and selling low. Traditional investment fundamentals still apply.

When it comes to buying stocks, there are a few key principles to keep in mind. First and foremost, it's important to know what hedge funds are investing in. These institutions have a wealth of resources and expertise at their disposal, and they often have a finger on the pulse of the market. Another key principle is to invest with a plan to hold for less than five years. This means you should have a clear idea of when you want to exit a particular investment and be prepared to pull the trigger when the time comes. It's also important to hyper-focus on a few great companies. Instead of spreading your money thin across a wide range of stocks, it's often better to put your eggs in a few baskets that you believe in.

Of course, there's always a degree of risk involved in investing. But as the old adage goes, nothing is the end of the world except the end of the world. So it's important to keep things in perspective and not get too caught up in short-term fluctuations. Another key principle is to invest at the maximum point of doubt and fear.

This means when the market is in a downturn and everyone is panicking, that's often the best time to buy. The key is to have the courage to act when others are too afraid to.

We've all heard the phrase "diversify your portfolio." This means investing in a variety of different asset classes in order to minimize risk and maximize returns. It also means avoiding the temptation to chase highs and instead, learning from your losses and making informed decisions to balance your risks.

In a world where cash loses value to inflation and taxes, it's important to create a mix of assets that can weather any storm. Ray Dalio, the renowned investor, created what he calls the "all-weather portfolio" to help investors navigate both bull and bear markets. A bear market is when stocks are trending downward, and a bull market is when they are rising.

On average, the stock market returns 9-10% a year over the course of more than a century. But for those who aren't risk-averse or just scared, bonds can be a more appealing option. Bonds are essentially a loan to a government or entity, whether it be a state, county, or corporation. They're considered a safer investment but with a lower return. One popular strategy for bond allocation is to subtract your age from 100 and invest that percentage in bonds and the rest in more aggressive assets. For example, if you're 40, you would invest 40% in bonds and 60% in stocks. This philosophy makes sense as you get closer to retirement.

Precious metals, hedge funds, and other alternative investments also have their place in a diverse portfolio. But it's important to remember that it's not about buying the things that go up and selling the things that go down. Market volatility can be likened to the yo-yo effect of walking upstairs. The Federal Reserve's quantitative easing program, or QE, has also played a role in market fluctuations. But one thing is for sure, holding on for the long term can help to build wealth. As the old saying goes, "Time in the market is more important than timing the market."

Nobody you-er than you

Once upon a time, the great Warren Buffett said the greatest investment you can make is investing in yourself. What does that mean? Well, it depends on where you are in life right now. Are you content with your current situation? Do you look in the mirror and see the best version of yourself? Would you let your daughter or son marry someone like you?

Management of business finances

Cash ain't king. Numbers on that balance sheet and bank statements are all that matters when we're talking business. You limit your empire if you don't have a solid accounting infrastructure and a paper trail. How do you expect to see how profitable you are if you are hoarding cash off the books? The cash loses value over time in your mattress, and it ain't safe there.

Your Barbershop needs a checking account, a tax account, a line of credit, and savings. I learned this while dating a CPA. She'd wanna spend time and do dinner dates during the early stages of the shop, and I just couldn't afford it. It took a great deal of humility to explain my dilemma and ask for her help. I had a personal checking account and a business checking account; that's it. I was cutting the clients, what I earned was going to my personal checking and I only deposited the booth rent from the Barbers for the business checking. Only two of our three chairs contributed to the business. Every now and then, I'd have to transfer funds from my personal account to the business to keep the ship sailing. My income was stable, and still carrying the business while the booth rent wasn't cash flow. Starting with new barbers who couldn't quite handle full rent, they were getting charged a fee that would increase over and hadn't matured yet. She suggested I take all of my income from haircuts and deposit that cash in the business account, and pay myself a salary weekly from the business account. It actually worked. So for the first few years, I paid myself only $500 a week and lived frugally even if I had earned $1500 from working. With this framework, we were able to make shop upgrades, handle unforeseen fees and show some revenue on our balance sheet. I took her advice to the extreme with the 2k monthly income and still didn't spare for leisure, causing her to find a more fiscally stable love interest.

When the Barbers were more consistent, I eventually increased our booth rent. Some barbers left abruptly, even though I showed love in the beginning by buying them shirts, business cards, and food with the money I didn't have and they didn't earn. That may be more of a misjudged character thing than a money thing, still correlated nonetheless. When managing your business finances, you need to be emotionless to a degree. If the numbers ain't right, they'll tell a story, and if it ends with you in the poor house, it'll be worse than Human Centipede. You can avoid this! Any operating costs, added features, or improvements need to be paid for by the people producing and receiving the instant benefit of it. Your business should be self-sustainable after you've been open for a while. The line of credit you have should only be used for income-producing assets or activities. Always remember you took the biggest risk for everyone by starting this business. They can add value that by putting some skin in the game and contributing a booth rent that makes sense for all parties involved. I only advise charging a higher rent when you have intentions to do right by your team and invest in them. You have to do what's best for them to make a living for your shop to be successful.

Once the shop switched to commission-based, we were able to get a full view of what we were grossing. Everyone's revenue besides their tips goes into our register, and we split it. For years during the booth rent era, we'd speculate on what the shop was doing overall. The commission business model works best when done correctly. It allows us to show banks and investors how profitable we are. I proposed a 60/40 split. It left a razor-thin margin for advancement on the Barbers' side. Our shop can't operate on less than 40% from the Barbers unless that 40% makes up more than 100% of your shop's operating expenses. If you're looking at your Profit and loss statements and your profit is less than 10%, you're wasting your time.

While in Miami, I met Gilbert, owner of High End Barbershop in Morristown, NJ. During our short talk, he explained he gives his Barbers 40% and the shop keeps 60%. Holy smokes Batman! They go no higher than 50/50. I won't share his numbers. Let's just say the shop is crushing it. We've chatted for hours since, and I've visited his shop and spoke with some of his barbers. A distinguishing quality of his shop is the guaranteed income a barber will earn starting out. 40% of what the shop earns is praiseworthy despite being in an affluent high cost of living area. Finance has been an intricate focus of his business. I trusted him to take a look at our statements, and he gave me some valuable advice on systems such as accounting for the Barber Shop.

When it comes to managing the finances of the business, it's important to have systems in place. This includes separating income, profits, owner/investor compensation, taxes, and operating expenses. Income is all the money that comes into the shop through services and products, and all deposits, whether card or cash, go here. Profits are a percentage of the income that is set aside for gains made from operations. We've used it for birthday gifts, team-building activities, profit sharing, and shop business trips. Owner/investor compensation is set aside for the founders and leaders of the business, and it operates as a quarterly dividend based on performance, productivity, and profitability. Taxes are estimated based on what needs to be paid to the state and federal governments. Last, our favorite, operating expenses include rent, utilities, insurance, liabilities, maintenance, and marketing, and it is used to keep the lights on in the shop. However, if you decide to split your shit up and pay your bills at your shop, it is your business. This is what has allowed us to operate with everyone being compensated fairly and our gas not getting cut off.

Retirement Planning

Retirement may seem far off for many self-employed barbers, but it's important to start preparing for it early on. Not only will this ensure a comfortable lifestyle in the future, but it will also give peace of mind and financial security.

Most shops don't have a retirement plan. It's usually the Barber or Salon professional's responsibility to handle their own retirement. Talk to some barbers, and they may not see that far in the future or know what to do when they get there. We can talk numbers, investment strategies, and look at charts, and it won't mean anything unless you can imagine what retirement looks like for you. Would you like to be comfortable and still work when you feel like it? Do you want to spend the rest of your life somewhere tropical? Do you want to buy a farm out in the countryside and BBQ with your family every weekend? More importantly, WHEN do you want to retire?! Don't say tomorrow, lol. The earlier you start saving for retirement, the more time your money has to grow. Compound interest can have a significant impact on the amount of money you have saved by the time you retire. Seriously it may take 10, 20, or 30 years depending on what you want and what your living expenses are today.

At some point, you'll have to add up what it costs to maintain your quality of life today. Include all of the bills, extra spending, and leisure. Once you have that amount then you know how much you'll have to make.

Actionable Steps

1. Differentiate between liabilities and assets: Remember the principles from "Rich Dad Poor Dad" about the difference between liabilities and assets. Take a look at your current financial situation and identify which items are assets and which are liabilities. Challenge yourself to increase your assets and minimize your liabilities.

2. Clean up your credit and build an emergency fund: Start by paying off your outstanding debts and negotiating payment plans with creditors. This will help improve your credit score and financial stability. Simultaneously, focus on building an emergency fund that covers at least six months of living expenses. Challenge yourself to save a specific amount each month until you reach your goal.

3. Invest in retirement accounts: Open an Individual Retirement Account (IRA) or Roth IRA, as these can provide tax advantages and long-term savings growth. Consult with a financial advisor to determine the best retirement account option for you. Challenge yourself to contribute regularly to your retirement account, aiming for the recommended 10-20% of your income.

4. Educate yourself on investments: Continue reading and learning about different investment options, such as stocks, index funds, and real estate. Understand the risks and potential returns associated with each investment type. Challenge yourself to start investing in a diversified portfolio, even if it's with small amounts initially.

5. Be cautious with speculative investments: While opportunities like cryptocurrencies, NFTs, and collectibles may seem tempting, approach them with caution. Don't let FOMO (fear of missing out) drive your investment decisions. Challenge yourself to thoroughly research and understand any investment before committing your funds.

6. Manage your business finances effectively: Implement proper accounting practices for your barbershop, including separate accounts for income, profits, taxes, and expenses. Seek advice from professionals to optimize your financial systems and maximize profitability. Challenge yourself to track your business finances meticulously and make informed decisions based on financial data.

7. Plan for retirement as a self-employed barber: Start preparing for retirement early by setting aside a portion of your income. Calculate your desired retirement lifestyle and determine how much you need to save to achieve it. Challenge yourself to create a retirement plan and contribute regularly towards it.

8. Imagine your retirement goals: Visualize what you want your retirement to look like and set specific goals. Consider factors such as where you want to live, the activities you want to engage in, and the financial security you desire. Challenge yourself to create a detailed retirement plan with clear milestones and action steps to make it a reality.

Remember, financial literacy and planning are ongoing processes. Stay committed to continuously educating yourself, adapting to changing circumstances, and making informed financial decisions.

NOTES

HOLDING COURT

"The last 10% it takes to launch something takes as much
energy as the first 90%."
—Rob Kalin, founder of Etsy

The Feds Watching

It may be hard to believe I came up in a barber world where
nobody cared about licenses. In all of my years, I've never
even witnessed a state inspection. Let's be clear here, I've
heard about them, and just because I've never experienced an
inspection doesn't mean you shouldn't be concerned about it.
I've worked in two different shops that were raided by Feds, yet
no State authorities ever checked our cleanliness or paperwork.
If Barbering regulations were criminal charges, a lot of shops
could be locked up on RICO. In NYS having a license can be the
difference between building a career and just cutting hair.

There were a few things I had to get right to be official. I held and renewed my Apprentice Barber License for several years (probably over a decade) before taking my Master's Exam seriously. The maximum amount of time you can hold that apprentice license is two years. The apprentice journey is my favorite route because it's the one I'm most familiar with. It allowed me to learn on the job pretty much. However, a majority of the barbers that panned out well in my shop were students who attended Barber Schools.

Recently while visiting Morocco, I found out about a NVQ (National Vocational Qualification) license that allows us to practice Barbering worldwide. With the emergence of Shear Share, an app that allows you to rent a chair anywhere (think Hair BnB), this may be worth looking into if you'd like to take your talents abroad. Have you ever wondered why your Barber License in Arizona means nothing in Alaska? Well, the founder of Shear Share, Dr. Tye Caldwell, has informed me that he's participating in a movement that's actively making progress towards getting our state licenses to be recognized nationwide.

Living off Experience

Despite my experience, the barber industry is regulated, and barbers must comply with many legal requirements to operate. These legal obstacles include licensing, insurance, and other regulations. While opening up our first space, insurance was one of the stipulations in the commercial lease. We had to be insured in case of some property damage or some accident for a worker and or a client. Unbeknownst to me at the time was the importance of being insured when we go out to the schools to do cuts for Saturday Academy. I've learned that more people are willing to do deals and business when they know you have your paperwork in order. It can be daunting to sit on the phone for hours, send emails, fax documents, or even pound on desks. If you want to call yourself a boss and conduct business, this is the part of it people rarely see or want to do, yet it keeps your ship afloat.

In order to operate in a barbershop, barbers must obtain a license from the state where they practice. This involves passing a written and practical exam and meeting requirements like completing a set amount of training hours. The license to own a shop and the license to practice Barbering are separate in NYS. The requirements and fees for licensing vary, depending on where you live in the US. I was well over my apprentice hours by the time I made the leap to take my master's exam, and everything I learned from the experience was NOT what I needed to know to pass it. I had to seek Barbers who successfully completed it to get prepared. I'll be honest; it was intimidating. There's no way in hell I could go out in the streets being the "Barber of the Buffalo Bills" and come back with an F! I practiced what I learned on clients until my exam date. I learned about health, sanitation, and compliance regulations like sterilization of equipment. A different way of hair washing, hot towel facials, shear, and razor techniques are needed to meet the state requirements. My test site was at a Barber Shop in Rochester, NY, and I brought my friend Tut with me to be my demo. He had long hair at the time and was very supportive. A free cut, road trip, and Popeyes were enough to sell the opportunity. The goal wasn't to give the most fly detailed crispy cut, it was to follow the instructor's directions; that's it. We all must have received that memo. There were a few catastrophes and chia pets in there. Watching the instructor look over his glasses in disbelief was one of those hilarious moments that gets funnier the longer you try not to laugh. I just did whatever he said to do and waited for his approval on each step. After weeks of uncertainty, my master's license was in the mail! It was a proud moment for me, my shop, and my grandma. She's always wanted me to do something positive, and to be able to make her smile was an accomplishment. Barbers of all skill levels slip through the cracks and get licenses every day, so before you pop the champagne, remember it doesn't mean you're God's gift to barbering. The license just means you can legally practice.

Agent nothing but a number

Starting a business is a journey filled with twists and turns. In December 2015, I had an intuition it was time to take my business to the next level, and I decided to file for an LLC. I did my research and found Legal Zoom, a company known for its comprehensive services, including franchise disclosures, trademarks, and more. With their easy-to-navigate website and helpful representatives, I completed the filing process in just 72 hours and received a big binder full of documents with the company name in gold letters.

Years later, while I was reviewing finances during a slow 4th quarter, I noticed a $600 withdrawal from LegalZoom. I reached out to the company to find out why they were charging me every year. I was shocked to discover that it was a "Registered Agent Fee." I was under the impression filing for an LLC was a one-time fee, but I soon learned that I only needed a registered agent during the registration process. I had been paying this fee for the past three years without realizing it.

I reached out to New York State and found out I didn't need to keep a registered agent, but LegalZoom never informed me of this, and I had to go through several steps to remove them from the paperwork. Sadly, they only reimbursed me for one year of the fee, and I lost $1000 over the first two years due to my lack of knowledge.

This experience taught me the importance of being informed and doing thorough research when making business decisions. While LegalZoom was convenient and easy to use, I learned it's essential to understand all the details, even after the initial filing process, to avoid unexpected fees and costs.

Paper Trail

Barber Shops must have insurance to protect the shop and the customers in case one of you practicing barbers slices an ear off. Liability insurance covers damages or injury, and workers' compensation insurance also covers job-related injuries or illnesses that prevent barbers from being able to perform. Most shops don't offer health insurance benefits, so it's on you to find a provider of a policy that works for you. Years ago, one of my close friends sold me insurance specifically for self-employed workers. They offered coverage for my hands and all the bells and whistles a barber would want, but guess what? None of the hospitals or doctors accepted it! So do your due diligence in reviewing your policy and your providers' strategic partners to make sure you are actually covered and can file claims. The last thing you want is another nonrefundable bill.

Zoning and building codes should be considered when you're looking for a location. I've been in talks to open a new location in a strip mall, which was a concern. We don't want to open our doors just to have Nappy Cutz set up across the street. Building codes are like hemorrhoids if you want to make renovations in a community of Karens. They'll send in spies to make sure you obtain permits and meet building and safety codes. That's been a setback for a few shops I've been in. Even at the time of this writing, a new vape shop in our neighborhood, Biggie Smokes, needs life after death and one more chance. They locked in a lease, made repairs, put up a sign, and stocked inventory; now they're petitioning for signatures due to not adhering to some law or code. Damn! I feel their pain. This is the same neighborhood where we had a wall vandalized several times by graffiti artists making our building look unprofessional. I called up some of the best painters in our city to do a mural for us. We're on the vegan, gluten-free side of town in a neighborhood known for culture. We added hip-hop flavor with our new red, white, and blue Fade in Full mural. Weeks later, it was covered by gray paint. You could've fried an egg on my face when I saw it. We actually paid close to $1000 for these artists to work for us, and I drove one to the store and watched him nerd out over paint before dropping an additional $500 at the art store. I took my anger campaign to the public with dozens of calls to community leaders and social media with no explanation for why our mural was covered up. Our mural was covered on the same day the city shut down shops for Covid before Christmas. What a nightmare! To raise money, I used a picture we had of the mural and put it on some hoodies we sold for $100 on Shopify. We sold enough to get a decent return... Not a bad idea, right? Well, I got a call from our eccentric artist. He spazzed on me and demanded our hoodie money because we were selling HIS art! Like really?! All of this may have been prevented if I had gotten the proper permits before the paint hit the wall. Or gave him a free hoodie...

F U pay me

We have federal and state employment laws related to wages, overtime pay, and discrimination. A safe working environment, fair wage benefits, and compliance with anti-discrimination are determined by laws. I got a crash course in this with our first manager, who was previously with Great Clips and brought administrative experience to our shop. An LGBT member well versed in the hiring processes and systems, the legal way. My line of questioning for potential candidates was too casual, to say the least. Our manager was able to smooth things out, handle some operations, do tedious staff stuff, and was very instrumental in finding our current location. Everything was white chocolate raspberry cheesecake until a non-shop-related injury managed them! Out of work indefinitely, they wanted me to forge documents saying we owed them back for their insurance claims. They argued, sent family members to see me, and even threatened to sue. Since we've never actually paid wages, I submitted all of the financial statements and documents available to their attorney with a letter stating I wasn't going to break the law for them. It's imperative you protect yourself even from people who know the laws. Some know the rules, try to find blind spots, and attempt to cheat the system at your expense. Owners must be aware of the risk of financial fraud and embezzlement. You would never let people play with your money, right? Treat the financial resources of the business the same way! Recordkeeping and financial reporting will protect you in situations like this. Also, accurate records of finances provide clarity for income, expenses, inventory, and filing regular tax returns. If you ever wanted to bring in investors, get a loan, or know the true value of your business, these records are like a report card showing your profitability and growth.

Riding Dirty

Uncle Sam needs to eat too. Federal, state, and local taxes can be handled quarterly or annually, depending on what's best for you. No lie; I'm claiming everything. For our first few years, I went to the same accountant to file taxes, since we were growing year over year. He was good overall, yet his firm was always busy with bigger clients, and I'd always file after April 15th, which is the federal deadline for taxes. Things were going well though, and everyone in the shop was making money. I was getting stamps on my passport and enjoying life once we made it through the first two years of building up. I once met a guy driving Uber after a flight who asked me some questions about taxes and how much we were earning and paying. Because he proved he was a CPA, I was forthcoming with the info. He claimed he could do my filing for half the price and save me on taxes. I salivated at the idea of fewer taxes, an accountant who was less busy, and no more late fees. About a week or so later, I was in his office, giving him the documents to file. He only told me how much I was paying and how much I owed him for his services which were as promised. Half of what I paid years prior. Fast forward to about eight months later, and I'm riding high and ready to purchase some real estate. The real estate agent just needed the tax returns to approve me. "Cool, sent it." Yeah, and days later, he explained to me that I couldn't be approved because of my income, and I'm like what? We made more money last year than ever! He said that's not what it says on your tax return. I felt like I missed a game-winning dunk when I processed what he was saying. I had never reviewed the return my Uber driver made. I opened up the PDF to see what actually was claimed there. Let's just say that if you judge our earnings by tax returns, we have "one bad year." That shit haunts me every time I wanna make a move regarding finance. And since it's been paid, there's no reason to open Pandora's box to appeal it. Not claiming everything you earn may have its advantages and disadvantages, even with all of your deductibles and loopholes. With this money game, if you play unfairly, there will be consequences. Think twice before you let Uber drivers file your taxes.

Paperwork

Legal challenges and disputes are the cost of being the boss. Suppliers, customers, employees, government agencies, bill collectors, and more are calling, and they only want to speak to whoever is in charge. Be prepared for legal processes or find knowledgeable people who know how to navigate it. Many of my troubles were due to not seeking legal advice. Coming from the hood, we only called attorneys when we caught cases. With several contracts and agreements in place, understanding the rights and responsibilities of all parties involved is a lot to handle in addition to your clients. If you have a good relationship with a lawyer, consider speaking to them, or an OG with experience can provide guidance on any issues that involve your paperwork. The last thing we want is for your career to be cut short over an accident, tax evasion, or fraud.

Actionable Steps

1. Licensing:
- Have you obtained the necessary license to operate as a barber in your state?
> - If not, research the licensing requirements in your state and take the necessary steps to obtain a license.
> - If you already have a license, ensure it is up to date and
renewed regularly.

2. Insurance:
- Do you have liability insurance to protect yourself and your clients in case of accidents or injuries?

- Review your insurance policy to ensure it provides adequate coverage and includes all necessary protections.
- Consider consulting with an insurance professional to assess your coverage needs and make any necessary adjustments.

3. Building Codes and Zoning:
- Are you familiar with your area's building codes and zoning regulations?

- Before opening a new location, research and comply with the building codes and zoning requirements specific to your industry.
- Obtain the necessary permits and approvals to avoid potential setbacks or legal issues.

4. Employment Laws and Compliance:
- Are you familiar with federal and state employment laws regarding wages, overtime pay, discrimination, and workplace safety?

- Review your hiring and employment practices to ensure compliance with these laws.
- If needed, consult with an employment lawyer or HR professional to ensure your business is meeting all legal requirements.

5. Taxes:
- Are you properly handling your business's federal, state, and

local taxes?

    - Consider consulting with a tax professional or accountant to determine the best tax filing schedule and maximize your deductions.

    - Review your past tax returns for accuracy and ensure that all income and expenses are properly documented.

6. Legal Documentation and Contracts:
- Have you established proper contracts and agreements with suppliers, customers, and employees?

    - Review your legal documentation to ensure it covers all necessary aspects and protects your interests.

    - If you encounter any legal challenges or disputes, seek legal advice from a qualified attorney to navigate the process effectively.

NOTES

ALL EYES ON ME

"Master the topic, the message, and the delivery." – Steve
Jobs

Gorillas love gold

Gorilla marketing is great for those who have unlimited marketing budgets. Throwing everything out there and hoping for the best. Billboards, radio, TV ads, posters, flyers, loyalty rewards, referral incentives, web pop-ups, sides of buses/cabs, sporting events, and more! I've seen small enterprises and even marketing firms blow the bag on all this brand awareness and then just disappear. For every Gorilla out there, there are some chimps too. Small businesses spend everything on supplies, payroll, etc., and leave nothing for the ad budget. Marketing is about creating awareness and connecting your brand message with your intended target group. It begins with the product or service, and it has to be good enough to talk about. Testimonials have to come easy for people. The story of your company and or your customers' experience with you needs to be shareable through conversation, online reviews, selfies, reposts or etc. The name, logo, colors, and copy should trigger emotion. Think about some of the big names and logos; you immediately recognize them when you see them. Some of my favorite logos are Nike, Target, McDonalds, and Pepsi. All of these are easy to identify without letters and words. That's why I decided to do our logo with the plug socket and two razors so that we can have a recognizable logo that doesn't need words. You can already predict what an experience will be like with a well-known brand. You can tell stories about your time there without thinking too hard about it. Marketing should be able to communicate your message and values effectively to those who you aim to attract. Big box whales, fast food corporations, and insurance have fueled what we know now as marketing. However, these are new times we live in with smarter consumers. They have more options, they've heard the jingles, and they see through the schemes, so if your product or service doesn't live up to what you portray in your ads, kiss your business and your budget goodbye.

The Seth Godin school of thought on marketing preaches you make your product or service remarkable, and it markets itself. My background in marketing stems from my time as a regional artist in the Western New York rap scene and most recently wearing the hat of "marketing guy" for our shops, so my approach to marketing our shop kinda felt like a mixtape and had that hip hop style approach.

We all have our own interpretation of what marketing is. I've met brilliant minds and some where on auto pilot. We had momentum going in year two before having a nationwide firm handle our marketing. Prior to that, I reached my peak of leveraging my popularity to drive the shop's Facebook Likes and Instagram followers. Making the leap to a marketing firm allowed professionals to build our website. A few bells and whistles we received were; they also wrote our copy, sent us a full quarter posting schedule list, and handled all of our reputation management. All we had to do was submit the content and keep cutting. Simple and easy! They added our logo to pics they posted on social media, created cool memes for us, and responded to every comment and review on Google. Also, our site was very SEO-friendly, which gave us good organic rankings on Google and Yelp. Search Engine Optimization makes a site more visible. I had already purchased several domain names for the shop (15+ different Fade in Full variations) from GoDaddy minutes after I locked in our LLC in 2015, so I figured a rep at "big market cartel" would contact me about it. Nope. "big market cartel" used a domain name they purchased for our website - FadeInFullBarbershop.net. Okay cool. No Biggie. No inquiry about who owns the name or any questions. I just promoted the name I purchased and forwarded all traffic toward FadeinFull. com to FadeInFullBarbershop.net. The site was pretty impressive; bright red, white, and blue colors, good copywriting, easy loading time, and our best photos. A different phone number?! Wait what?! I called up our account manager about this, and they said they were using a number they could track stats from. Oh okay...

I guess that makes sense. I can see the reason for this. However, were we going to be privy to those stats and data?! How were we going to adjust and remarket based on that phone data?! I asked some very good questions. I was between a hungry group of barbers who wanted to service people and a marketing team that was dancing to the beat of 12k per year. A whopping expense for a 4-chair North Buffalo Barbershop in 2017-18. Our relationship with them was pretty smooth for the most part until…. I asked more questions.

It's yours

Along the journey of self-improvement, some fat was trimmed off the friend circle, and some loyal clients became opps. I recall wanting to get some pictures of these individuals removed from our website just to be informed I'd reached my limit of adjustments to our website. Excuse me?! I only have a set amount of times I can make alterations?! Huh? Okay, no problem. Whatever it costs extra to change the pics, do it. I didn't think it'd be often that I'd need to change things, so if it were a fee to do it, I didn't complain. But then it seemed to happen again and again where I'd have to make some alterations or call some audibles on their 12-week posting schedule to meet fees and restrictions. The last straw was when I wanted to make our website more practical. We had a cool site, but it did nothing! You couldn't buy anything there. You couldn't book there. You couldn't apply for a job there. My first ever zoom calls were around this time with the reps from the "big market cartel," they could sense my frustration through my cheap Webcam when they dropped the bomb on me that they own our website. What?! They designed it, so they own it. I wanted to throw my laptop out of my third-story apartment window. They were paid a fee to build it, yet they weren't willing or able to meet my requests. They didn't have the resources to handle this. They made me feel like I was insane; like why would people book online when they could call? With Uber, Lyft, and Airbnb on the rise, it was a matter of time before we'd be making a leap to a digital age of scheduling, and I wanted to be on the forefront of the movement.

Before severing ties with our huge nationwide marketing firm, I took a look at all of our emails and agreements from the firm. The contracts did state what they explained to me during our last call; I failed to notice. It's common for us to sign on with terms and conditions and not read the fine print. All of the legal jargon and mumbo jumbo is where they get us. I grabbed some marketing books and social media books around this topic to learn as much as I could, so I knew what questions to ask any potential candidates. I needed to know everything and know it extremely fast. I kept our "big market cartel" built site while interviewing with more marketing firms. The cost to upgrade to a new firm that would meet my standards was too expensive for us at the time, so I took matters into my own hands and decided to use what I learned from them to go the distance and control everything on my own. I ended the contract, and as promised, they wiped their version of our site clean from the internet without an option to buy.

Me against the web

I discovered some incredible books on marketing, social media, and campaign management. I found thought leaders and influencers like Seth Godin, Gary Vee, Tai Lopez, and Billy Gene, who shifted paradigms for me in regard to promo. In my quest, I had brilliant ideas for how to take the barbershop to new levels. I envisioned us becoming more interactive, more personality online, and more videos for our social and website. I was dead set on doing long-form YouTube content for every barber telling their story and clipping the best clips for Instagram and Facebook. I formatted the clips for stories on Instagram, and the ones for regular posts on Facebook. This was years before the same content could be utilized across all platforms. I decided on videos that captured Before and After haircuts with cool transitions, and dope beats playing in the background— 30-sec visuals with some digital graphics on our logo. I even went on Fiverr and started getting voiceovers for the videos with scripts written by me. All of this footage was shot using my phone camera, and looking back at all of this work I was doing, I realized I was driving myself crazy. I've always been the type that would use whatever resources were available to make things happen. Some barbers appreciated it more than others. I spent more time reading and editing than anything else in my spare time. My ads were running but had no real strategy on how to check the insights and analytics. I exhausted money, energy, attention, and time while gathering a wealth of knowledge and experience. My style of "marketing" was effective in attracting barbers to the shop and customers. The final destination for all of our leads was a website designed on Wix by my girlfriend, Kelly; I've been updating that same site ever since.

While shooting, editing, running ads, and consuming marketing via books and media, I had an idea of launching a subscription box for barber supplies. The journey of networking and sourcing capital for my side project, the Barber Box, was how I discovered Squire. Squire created a booking platform for Barbershops. The tech startup won a local Shark Tank-type contest, and the software changed the game. Thanks to Squire we're able to track our stats, use our contact list, set our schedule, and handle POS and payroll. Most importantly, people can book online.

Online booking allowed us to start building funnels. Our previous ads led to people calling in, which was a little annoying, to be honest. With online booking, we could avoid having to stop a cut to answer the phone, and people could find a time and professional that works best for them.

No way out

Now Rusell Brunson is the authority on funnels. Funnel is basically your lead generation tool—the journey your customer makes to a purchase. There are many different ways your customers make it through; it may start with a Google search, a youtube ad, or a dope post on social media; maybe even a QR code. What I learned is you want to ultimately minimize the clicks to conversion for leads online. Meaning when someone clicks a book now button on social media, that's all they want to do, and that process should be as easy as possible. You may deal with some people who are reluctant to enter card info or some who are computer illiterate; honestly, this isn't for them. That late blooming, last-minute bunch still uses rotary phones. The forward thinkers and early adopters of things are the people that are going to embrace change and make things easier for you. People with bank accounts and cards limit the money issues, and if they don't show, it's easier for you to enforce your cancel policies because you already have the payment in your system- less headaches for you and your customers. It makes it easier to conduct business on both sides; The people need to book, and the barbers need to be available to cut.

True story

There's an art to marketing. Often I go to a barber's social media channel, and there is a flood of haircuts on the page with little about the person or the shop. We learn nothing about who they are or what they stand for. The true art of marketing is in conveying your vibe and values through pictures and text. This may be your customer's first impression of you. If you're online bragging about being the best, you are basically playing the hero in your own story. Sure, that works for motivating yourself; however, it's not so effective in attracting people. Every barber thinks they're the best, and every shop feels they're the best. Make your customers feel like the hero. They should feel like they're the best because you're assisting them in their journey. In every story, we have a hero with a goal, a guide, and an antagonist. In our case, the antagonist would be the bad barbers or the bad shops. The goal for the hero is the good cut and service, and you're the guide to get them there. A great example of this concept is The Lion King. Simba is the hero, and the goal is to be king. The antagonist is his evil uncle Scar, and the guide is Rafiki, the orangutan who reminds him he is royalty and gives him the inspiration to take on his uncle. Better yet, here's another example: Rocky & Creed. These movies have the same formula every time. The main hero, the boxer, has a goal to become a champion or remain the champion. The antagonist is the current title holder or hot new contender challenging the champion. The guide is the trainer who brings our hero back to life with a beloved training montage that prepares our hero to beat his opponent in the end, reaching the goal. Great! Now that we got that. How do you position yourself as a guide? Pictures of yourself actually doing the cuts! Yes, action shots of you providing the service. Whoever is in the chair shouldn't look like their puppy just died! In your caption is where you highlight the pain point you aim to fix with a question. Has your barber left town without letting you know?! Need someone reliable? They have no choice but to notice this if they've ever been through that before, and when they see how professional you are in your picture or video, you've got their attention. They have a takeaway that you're the guide they've been looking for.

Dream Team

Once you are a busy barber or an owner running a shop, it'll be taxing on your time to handle marketing unless you are passionate about it. Trust me, I know this, and I've interviewed many firms to take on the job in these past few years. Barbers and Shops have different marketing needs. Hiring a firm was one of the best decisions ever for the shop. Learning about marketing was great not only for me but also so I was knowledgeable enough to not let these people lose me with all types of keywords and phrases to sell me a service that I didn't need. We can get down and dirty to what you will actually need. For barbers, you want to have a memorable style on your page on social media, so you need some type of common theme with your post that communicates who you are to your potential customers besides haircuts. If they are coming to your page and it's just a bunch of pics of other people and none of you on there, that's kinda wack. Your content should express who you are and establish consistency with a posting schedule! Remember how we wait on our favorite shows to be released or an important sporting event?! Your content should be that way! We should expect you to give advice on one day, show a cut another day, show your interest in a client, and go live and connect. You're building an audience. It's a job, I know… If you have time to watch everyone else or your board around the shop, that is your time to go through that gallery! Look at those old pictures of cuts. Make content about that! Step out of the zone and let the world know who you are and the real authentic you will attract the people. I've even seen some people that aren't comfortable on camera; that's fine, you still have a voice. This barber game is extremely saturated, and everyone can cut so you have to set yourself apart from the crowd.

Hire a firm for the shop. Not just any marketing firm; can the firm leverage clout to bring influencers to your shop? How often will they post organically for you? Are they going to write the copy and respond to them for you? Do they make reels and shorts? Are you going to be responsible for creating your own content and taking your own pictures? Do they have a photographer on staff that can take high quality pictures for you? Are they local and know your market? Are they able to use your data to calculate acquisition costs? Does the cost of hiring this firm eat more than 13% of your gross revenue? If so, can the shop handle it?

A real question!
Can your staff handle the potential rush of customers?!

Actionable Steps

1. Branding and Messaging:
- Have you defined your brand identity, including your name, logo, colors, and brand story?
    - Ensure that your branding elements evoke emotion and are easily recognizable.
    - Review your brand messaging to ensure it effectively communicates your values and resonates with your target audience.

2. Online Presence and Website:
- Do you have a professional website that showcases your services, highlights customer testimonials, and provides essential information?
    - Evaluate your website's usability, loading speed, and

mobile responsiveness.

- Consider implementing online booking functionality to make it easier for customers to schedule appointments.

3. Social Media Marketing:

- Are you utilizing social media platforms effectively to promote your barber shop?

- Create a content strategy that includes a mix of haircut showcases, behind-the-scenes footage, customer stories, and engaging posts.

- Consistently post content and interact with your audience to build a strong online presence.

4. Lead Generation and Funnels:

- How are you generating leads and converting them into customers?

- Implement lead generation strategies such as offering promotions, referral incentives, or creating informative content to capture potential customers' contact information.

- Develop a funnel that guides potential customers through the journey from awareness to conversion, minimizing the steps required for them to book an appointment.

5. Local Marketing and Partnerships:

- Are you leveraging your local community to expand your reach?

- Collaborate with complementary businesses or local influencers to cross-promote and reach new audiences.
- Participate in local events or sponsor community initiatives to increase brand visibility.

6. Hiring a Marketing Firm:
- If you decide to hire a marketing firm, consider the following:
    - Research firms that have experience in the barber industry and understand your target market.
    - Inquire about their services, including content creation, social media management, influencer collaborations, and organic posting.
    - Discuss pricing and ensure that the cost aligns with your budget and revenue goals.
    - Clarify their approach to data analysis and tracking key metrics to measure the effectiveness of their campaigns.

7. Content Creation and Differentiation:
- How are you differentiating yourself from other barbers or shops in your area?
    - Experiment with different types of content, such as videos, before-and-after transformations, educational posts, or stories that showcase your personality and expertise.
    - Constantly innovate, find unique ways to engage your audience, and set yourself apart from the competition.

SEEING IS BELIEVING

"You should set goals beyond your reach, so you always have something to live for."
—Ted Turner

Evolution is a constant force that drives life forward, and without a long-term vision, one remains limited while the world continues to move forward without them. As a man above 40, I've experienced the world evolve. The world I grew up in was vastly different from the one I live in today - there was no such thing as Wi-Fi, on-demand shows, ride-sharing, or twenty different kinds of Oreos. In my early years, there were still "Black Barber Shops' ' and "White Barber Shops," and if a white man walked into a black barbershop in the 80s or 90s, he would be immediately assumed to be law enforcement or lost.

Kaleidoscope

I wanted to create a barbershop where anyone could get their hair done, no matter their race, and where barbers could relate to anyone who walked in. So, when I decided to open my own barbershop, people expected it to be a "black shop." By definition, that wouldn't be wrong, but I had a different vision. This was met with pushback and ridicule from some, but I stayed true to my vision. I hired whoever had skills and would fit the culture of the shop. That included Black, white, Latino, gay, transgender, young, and old barbers, even creating shirts with our logo in multi-colored designs to reflect the diversity of our team.

Hiring a white barber wasn't a big deal after a few came and went. The real game-changer was when Lady Barber Meg joined us. I first met her girlfriend in the gym and was impressed by her short haircut, so I asked who did it. After a brief conversation, Meg's girlfriend, Liz, brought her in to meet me. Meg was working as an apprentice in a small-town barbershop, but Liz felt she could do better. Meg started following our content on social media, and thereafter, joined our team. Her arrival caused a stir, as people were surprised to see a white, lesbian female barber in our "black shop." There were some who gave her a chance and some who walked out if she was the only one available. However, she proved herself and quickly became an integral part of our team.

Meg and I learned a lot about one another while we were roommates during covid. Professionally she taught me about shear usage, and our apprenticeship became a bond between two people from different cultures and backgrounds who shared a common passion and vision. My experience with her has shown me that we can welcome people from diverse backgrounds and of different preferences into a world often perceived as misogynistic or toxic. Over the years, we have attracted a wide range of customers, and I'm proud of the diverse team we've built at Fade in Full Barbershop.

Leaders and Followers

A smooth day at the shop is everyone smiling, making money, feeling well, and we're on time. A job well done is wrapping up the day and recapping with the last few barbers left and an insider or two. We unpack areas of improvement and discuss ideas of what's to come in the future. Growing a shop into a company is a vision many owners have, yet can't bring to fruition. Is it a lack of vision? Sometimes I wonder - if I had stayed at past shops, would there be an endgame for me? I made tons of money in other shops, yet something deep within me caused me to want to leave to seek a greater purpose. We can become jaded with work without dreams that motivate us and drive us. Ending a barber career with lasting impact is a driving force that guided me this far and even towards writing this book.

The life cycle of a barber rarely ends in a decorated hall of fame retirement. We start, learn how to cut, cut, and keep cutting until we can't cut anymore. Dreams of being a Billionaire Barber might sound audacious. How often do we hear about a shop growing into an enterprise? Or one of our neighborhood shops becoming a global brand that goes public? For most of us, it's every man for themselves. Shops compete against one another and die by the price. Or like Sean Thompson always tells me, "die behind the chair." Sean and I have a quirky relationship. He may not recall our first time in the same room; it was '07 when he called a meeting to unify the Buffalo Barbers in a commission like something you'd see in The Wire or The Godfather. I hope he NEVER remembers the second time. At a hair show, "some" guy stormed the stage, snatched the mic from the host, yelled, threw chairs, and got pepper sprayed by security! Fast forward to five years, and Fade in Full has momentum. We eventually crossed paths in NYC at Barbercon. Seans' reputation, ownership, and work in education had transcended. He blazed a trail by organizing trade shows, and many barbers from his classes were heavy hitters. Our talk at Barbercon marks the beginning of a kinda informal mentorship. I valued his wisdom so much that I'd pull up early Saturday mornings to his shop with donuts to speak with him for a few minutes. A few times, I've caught him working before I opened up my shop, and he'd still be there working after I closed up! He's older than me, so I asked about the end of our life cycle, and he simply said, "As soon as you get in this game, you gotta find a way to get out of this game. If you gotta cut hair to survive, you gonna have a problem. I don't care how much we love it, we all gonna break down, and we all gotta have an exit plan." He shared with me what may be the best exit plan for him. I have no doubt that he'll make it happen since he mentioned his plans for his current shop to me during our talk at Barbercon. Since that day, we've both relocated and kept in touch. To be honest, I wish I'd been listening to him much earlier.

Pieces of a plan

No Grease is a great example of an exceptional long-term vision. The family-owned barbershop franchise was founded and is operated by 3 Brothers in Norfolk, Virginia. They've been successfully empowering barbers and entrepreneurs through a high-quality service and franchise model. While other salons and barbershops have struggled to establish a brand and solid framework, No Grease has been able to expand to 20 locations in the south and continues to grow. Rob Baxter was the first person to ever mention this to me when he and his nephew proposed a partnership to me for Iconz, a reputable Buffalo-based Barbershop. I wasn't ready to start a shop on my own, so it sounded exciting to be a part of a full-service spa for men. Iconz was launching their 4th location, and it was nothing I'd ever seen before. Fresh new stations and barber chairs. An upstairs area with a bar, sauna, shower room, locker room, and three massage suites in a growing neighborhood. In hindsight, the space was esthetically pleasing, yet the partnership lacked a solid business plan and proper structure from the gate. All agreements were verbal, and most of them were between the family before I was invited. After a year in, I was simply renting a booth, making contributions with no return, and had no true ownership. The fulfillment tank was empty. I was churning and burning, never receiving one passive dollar there. I was stressed tf out with several areas of my life, including this chaotic and tense work environment. Truthfully my Iconz experience could be its own book titled the "48 laws of Sour." We parted ways in 2015.

Three years later, a No Grease Franchisee made a surprise visit to me at Fade in Full! Apparently, he was following us on YouTube, liked what he saw, and booked an appointment to talk to me. He explained to me how their company qualifies franchisees based on liquidity and net worth as well as experience in hair or leadership. They've calculated start up costs, projected gains, and provided assistance with team building and marketing. After I picked my jaw off the floor, I picked his brain a little more. I couldn't help but recall flashbacks of every unmet demand at Iconz. I didn't have much input or influence, and I wasn't aware that we weren't following the No Grease blueprint. That had to be a key factor in why our "location" failed. I don't share many stories about that time since the highlights were far and few; the lowlights made the news. That era had the presentation of long term vision. It had the potential, and we lacked discipline and execution. I contributed to the downfall once I knew the ship was sinking. I wasn't a leader, and I didn't know then what I know now. I could have done more to challenge the leadership. After hearing about how organized No Grease was, I began to do more research on the company and its founders to find clues on what I could do to protect the interests of Fade in Full.

First Down

Leadership and long-term vision are essential for success in any industry, including barbering. As an experienced barber and owner of my own shop, I've come to understand the importance of having a clear vision and being able to inspire and motivate my team towards our goals.

My friend, Coach Rome, is a great example of a leader with a long-term vision. As the Phil Jackson of little league football, he has achieved great success through his visionary leadership. His little league teams have winning streaks and several championships, all thanks to his ability to make decisions that benefit the staff, kids, parents, and organization.

Despite limited resources and few role models, Coach Rome has managed to turn his life around and become a respected pillar of our community. He has always been supportive of my barbershop, sending referrals and supporting me no matter how far away I was.

When I recently asked him about his approach to long-term vision, his answer surprised me. He takes things one day at a time and focuses on helping others reach their goals. This approach makes sense when one is doing the right thing, and it's a testament to his ability to judge character and intuition.

What I've learned from Coach Rome is that if you have righteous intentions, a solid playbook, and the right team, you can focus on one thing at a time. This consistency will compound, and success will follow. As he says, "I can tell you everything I ever did bad in football because the good outweighs the bad so much."

As barbers and business owners, we can learn a lot from how leadership and long-term vision is applied to sports. By staying true to our vision and consistently providing quality service, we can build momentum and achieve our goals. With the right attitude and work ethic, anything is possible.

Saved by the Bell

Young barbers are set to revolutionize the barbering industry. I had an opportunity to witness their potential firsthand at the Harkness Center, a local vocational high school packed with young talent and energy. Mrs. Reinard, an experienced barber and cosmetology instructor, invited me to speak to her students, and I was one of three called in to speak, one of two to open and run a shop. The students were eager to learn about what it's like in the real barber world, and I gave it to them with no filter.

The students didn't just limit their questions to what inspire' me to become a barber. They were genuinely interested in the process of opening and owning a shop. They took notes and seemed to identify with my stories of overcoming hardships, including my time in jail, and connected with my authenticity during my journey. The engagement and enthusiasm from them were inspiring to me, and hearing about how some of them are already cutting for money in their teens is impressive.

During my time at the Harkness Center, I met two particularly remarkable young Barbers among the class, Elias and Cold Cuts, also known as Jason. Elias, whose father was a barber, displayed exceptional skills and a burning desire to open his own shop at some point. Elias even came to visit me with his dad at Fade in

Full on one Saturday morning. We chopped it up for about three hours. Cold Cuts, on the other hand, shared his ambitious plan to open up his own shop within the next five years. He envisioned a space with the sharpest Barbers who could cater to any client's needs, including dying hair, and his mom, who does hair is also a part of his vision. Cold cuts was also on camera, claiming that he cuts better than I do, with over a thousand career cuts at 16. I love his confidence.

When they asked me about opening up, I reminisced about my early days, and they brought me back to the pivotal moment when peeking through the window of an empty space was how I saw all of the possibilities. I explained to them how I transformed that space, painted the walls, redo the floor and installed ceiling fans before I even considered buying chairs. The story resonated with them, and they understood the importance of having like-minded people sharing the vision of a shop before starting the journey.

Sean Thompson, a revered educator/shop owner, was a guest speaker, and I asked the students what was one of their takeaways from him, and they all said, "you're not a real Barber if you're not doing everything". Sean ignited their passion for mastering several different services and being well-rounded as a barber. I didn't disagree with what Sean was telling them. In theory, it is correct. I believe Sean has great intentions and is molding the next generation; however, I emphasized that they need to specialize before they generalize.

141

My time at the Harkness Center was an unforgettable experience. It reaffirmed my commitment to a lifelong journey of growth and learning. Witnessing their enthusiasm and hunger for knowledge filled me with hope for the future of this industry. The emergence of this new class marks a significant shift in the dynamics of the trade. Their new perspectives, innovative ideas, and determination are transforming the landscape. I believe that these young talents will reshape our industry and inspire others to push past our existing boundaries and challenge some of the norms for a new level of excellence.

Fresh Canvas

I seem to be at a crossroads with our expansion plan. Lex, our fiery young barber, found a commercial space near her home that we checked out recently. We met with a broker who handles tenants for an out-of-state company that owns the space; right now, it's empty. No tenants, walls, or anything. The mixed-use space is attractive and needs a buildout. Finding capital and obtaining permits to build a new shop has been in slow motion during the holiday season and harsh weather. Meetings began in November, and February breezed by without us pouring in concrete yet. My friend, Aaron, has been handling most of this thus far and connected me with his colleague, Rob, who does construction. Rob has done a build-out for a salon owner Jamie. They invited me to see Jamie's hair salon Canvas and her nail bar Polished. Both are located close to the same strip mall in an affluent suburban village.

The detail and cleanliness of Canvas were breathtaking. We

sat and enjoyed coffee in her waiting area while the 20-year vet explained her business model. Rob showed me all of the technical details of his customizations while Jaime explained the functionality. The salon operates on booth rent. Beauticians have individual prices based on skill level & demand. The 1100 Sq ft space can facilitate wedding parties and packs four salon stations, two sinks, a dispensary with dryers, a break room, a waiting area, and an office. Floating mirrors are backed by illuminating lights, and everything that isn't in use is out of sight and tucked away in an area built by Rob. They offer coffee or wine free of charge to the guests—a pretty tight-run operation. The age range of the workers in the hair salon is 30-50, while the nail salon is 20-30. I asked her what it's like to deal with two different businesses, two different staff, in two different generations. She put a lot of emphasis on presence and not bringing work home; two rules that I break religiously. I work on admin tasks at home since my "desk" at my shop is in a basement with no windows, heat, or decor. Jaime highly recommended I have an office space. "You'll ruin your marriage and your life. It's important to leave work at work. It's also nice to have a space where you can talk to your employees and have a closed door conversation. You can't do that in the breakroom. You can't do that on the floor, and when you start taking them to a coffee shop, the message gets deluded. Having a space to really connect and deliver a message is important. Obviously, you need to have a safe space to maintain some sanity. You're still creating a presence as a leader and an owner by being on-site whether you're on the floor cutting hair or you're in your office." I agreed while we migrated one door down to a break room with a new washer & dryer conveniently placed underneath all of the HVAC stuff; I almost didn't notice it. Jaime doesn't believe in big break rooms. This one is smaller than she'd like; however, every full-time renter has a locker. The break room serves as a space where the workers can chill and eat away from the clients.

They don't like mess. "It's gotta be organized, and it's gotta be clean because your clients see that." During covid, when everyone thought the moon would sneeze a particle on the earth and we'd all get sick, her clients wrote letters and texts saying they would eat off her floor! She's really proud of that, and a lot of it has to do with extreme organization of space. Visiting with Jaime refreshed my sense of urgency. Once I explained a few details about my potential second location, she said, "Do it!". There's no doubt that we'd be able to design a new shop customized for premium customer experience. That part of the vision is easy for the visionary. A grandiose vision requires belief from many people and a united effort.

America's Most Daunted

Sometimes you have to ask yourself why, and the answer may motivate you. It also can discourage you depending on how real you are with yourself. Upon my expansion crusade, a month-long trip, and work-from-home days, there was a change of heart at Fade in Full with customers and staff. More than half of my clients went to other shops, overall numbers were declining monthly, quality control dipped, and I was HR, putting out one fire after another- personally and professionally. Once the ship has some holes and ain't floating right, we're all asking ourselves, "Why are we doing this?!" Part-time barbers were doing full-time numbers, and Full-time barbers were doing part-time numbers. Some were considering switching careers. One may have hit the 'Harry Powder' and thought he WAS me in my absence! A better question to ask is, "Should we really expand?!" The answer is very layered. Motivating or intimidating, depending on how you see it.

I feel charged thinking about helping someone reach a higher level, something more than just a barber. However, if they don't really want it, don't share the vision or make the effort; it's gonna fail! Patrick Bet-David inspired me to build the right team before mastering a strategy to scale. The mental see-saw of 'scale or sale' begins in my mind and ends with my team. Depending on the day or issue the team might get seen or sawed. I started this journey hoping it wouldn't be born alone and die alone. I have potential running mates and haven't done enough to make my tasks transferable to them yet. Even if they were ready, one shop leaves us with a not-so-competitive salary cap. Different combinations of staff throughout the years got max effort based on my level of knowledge, resources, and experience at the time. Buying them business cards and making promo videos when I was fresh off my mixtape peak drove performance in the beginning.

Over time I became a C-E-all with no personal time to spare! When I wasn't behind the chair, I'd be reading books, attending business conferences, and meeting successful people from various industries to gain insight. Now I'm looking at our one-shop operation through a new lens with the potential for exponential growth! "*My* ''new lens though; it's not quite the view my team got. They may see a business conference as a recreational trip; new barber chairs are expendable, like old barber chairs. Football is light-years better than any book! I'll see our ad campaigns and think about the cost of customer acquisition. They may only see walk-ins (that aren't as important as their appointments). Social media, in my mind, is a lead generator; for them, it may be a place to catch laughs and connect with friends. A book club in our shop for kids?! An opportunity to leave and handle what's important to them. People have lives and families. Their own interests. Their own vision. I get it.

One meeting ripped stitches out of that wound. I've created manuals with the technical stuff I've learned in an attempt to enlighten my group. It features our stats, systems, and projections; fifty pages or less, not as dense as this book you're reading now. Our manual included full-color pictures, unlike this one you're reading now. The recent edition was dispersed, and no one brought it to our meeting! I had gift cards ready to award whomever did, since I didn't say it was mandatory to do so. Maybe barbers don't care about books, or the Barber writing this one needs a reality check. They didn't ask me to create this. Why did I really do it?! Most of what I know is from experience or reading and executing what I learned. It was an attempt to present what was never available to me. Sharing the info in a way that I wish it was shared with me. The goal is for us to grow together. For those of you who see value here, you may have a competitive edge over the group. They have me so close that my intentions may be blurred, misunderstood, or not urgent. Most barbers are self employed at heart and wanna move to the beat of their own drum. Here I come complicating things with all this business stuff.

Conducting our meetings in boardrooms, tracking our progress on whiteboards, and expecting continued growth. There may be moments where we find ourselves doing what we think people need, when really it might only be what WE want. Pondering on this, I recalled a story 50 cent shared. G-Unit had a meeting after the success of album sales, world tours, video games, sneakers, and clothing lines. All of the members were there, and Fif was the only one wearing G-Unit clothing. Undoubtedly, we care for each other, work together, and share a vision. The truth is, people may not see it the same as you do, and that's fine as long as you never lose sight.

Shady Aftermath

Sacrifices will be made. A diverse team and a family-friendly shop alienated some true friends that held me down in the streets. It led me toward a different network and prosperous opportunities. Going through growing pains allowed me to see rivals as idols in the industry. We're working together instead of tearing one another down. Partnering with an organization caused immediate setbacks yet pushed me towards true ownership. Letting go of clients gave me time to work on more urgent tasks to improve the shop overall. Wins and losses get stacked with the choices we make. The wins outweigh the losses when you stay dedicated to your vision no matter what. Many of us struggle to get past avoiding making mistakes and caring too much about what people think—playing to 'not lose' instead of 'playing to win.' Everybody won't be your cheerleader, help, or want you to win. In the words of the late Kobe Bryant, "boos don't block dunks." He didn't allow spectators, defenders, or weak teammates to stop him from practicing. They didn't control his routine, break his spirit or compromise his vision of being the best, and winning built his confidence. Losing built his character, and character is the most valuable thing we can build in order to win in life. The mamba practiced six hours a day, six days a week! Even during the off season. Have you ever been that dedicated? We're still talking about practice, not the actual game! Neither one of us is Kobe Bryant. We are who we are, and who we are ain't who we were. Today begins forever. A new beginning of who we're meant to be. Embrace making the leap forward despite where you are in your life. Your character, personal habits, and work ethic is the path. Your vision is the light at the end of the tunnel. Whether you're the barber looking to do a certain amount of heads in one day, open a shop, or open several shops and a school, the first step is to manifest it with your vision. See it, believe it, then achieve it.

DYE TRYING

"I am already a product" - Ross Perot

It's rare you see many products in the average Barbershop. If you do, it's limited to some merch or vending machines. We sold chips and cookies, but opening a supply store and offering hair products was always a goal. Going inside a salon and seeing a fully stocked product section feels like second nature. I once worked in a salon with Barbers, and they were moving so much product that they kicked the barbers out to make more room for inventory! Salons' Clients are conditioned to buy things from the experts that handle their hair. Meanwhile, in the barber shops, haircuts are the bread and butter; that's it. Growth lies in products, my people- Products for those extra services we should be providing, products for clients with dirty hair and dandruff. Products for your one guy with thinning hair on top, products for your other man with the nestle crunch bumps under his beard. Think for a moment, and you'll realize most of your clients have unmet needs for hair and skin. If they are asking for a solution, why are you sending that money somewhere else? According to market research, skin care is projected to be an 18 Billion dollar industry by 2027! And you mean to tell me some of us are only slapping on a quick cut and some oil sheen?! We can do so much better. I know you gonna have some customers that feel like they don't want extra service or think they are too tough for hot towel facials but fuck that!!!! We gotta revolutionize this shit together, regardless.

We set the trends

I was eager to dive into the world of product development, fueled by a mix of excitement and blind ambition. Without much forethought, I impulsively purchased display cases from eBay, which I assembled with the help of my supportive friend, G, on a drunk Thanksgiving Eve. The glass showcases would remain empty until my return from a road trip.

Determined to fill the display cases for retail, I tapped into the relationships I had cultivated during the time of my mixtape venture. It turned out that most of the stores where I sold my music also carried beauty supplies. It was advantageous that they offered me existing inventory at a slightly higher price than wholesale, which sufficed for a while. However, it was during a routine haircut session with my friend, Sam, that the tide shifted. Curiosity got me, and I inquired about how he had managed to establish his own beauty supply store. He revealed that he was on the verge of closing it down! It was at that moment that I discovered my golden opportunity - Sam introduced me to a larger supplier who had everything I needed. But there was a catch; they had a minimum order requirement, and I had to obtain a secret code to access their exclusive site. Unveiling this whole new world of possibilities meant jumping through a few legal hoops of getting a license to sell products, and that was pretty simple. Around this time, conversations with Sam inspired me to explore ways to make our shop stand out and consider selling products alongside our services. Most shops weren't doing it, and we needed the extra revenue. Chips and cookies didn't cut it or fulfill a real need related to hair. During my idle moments, a brilliant idea hit me- The Barber Box, a monthly subscription box with essential barbering supplies like neck strips, razors, disinfectant sprays, and aftershaves. Initially, I envisioned variations of the box for customers, including travel-size shampoos and toys for children, encouraging healthy hair care practices with newsletters. I saw it as a hair-happy meal for industry insiders and high-maintenance clients. However, a brainstorming session with Mr. Wes led us to realize that the true potential was in catering to barbers exclusively. My passion and drive for this project were immeasurable, prompting me to invest my time, money, and efforts without hesitation. I even approached friends for investment, but whatever, they declined, and I kept going. It was during this period that my girlfriend introduced me to Marilyn at the SBDC (Small Business Development Center).

Marilyn, a true game changer, became an invaluable resource on this tumultuous journey. Armed with my plans, projections, and notes stored within a red five-star notebook, I went into her office seeking guidance. She provided me with invaluable support, leading me towards numerous opportunities that I would have otherwise missed. With her assistance, I was now in the room with Venture Capitalists and pitching my idea to the power movers of our tech world in western New York.

Undeterred by initial difficulties, I launched an all-out promotional campaign for The Barber Box. Advertisements, videos, and even contests were employed in my relentless pursuit of customers. I traveled tirelessly to various barber shops and dialed countless numbers, hoping to drive sales. I lost clients that took it personally that I was allocating all efforts towards this. Unfortunately, despite my best efforts, success eluded me during our global pandemic of 2020. It became evident that my execution fell short, ultimately resulting in the demise of that project.

However, this setback became a powerful lesson etched into my entrepreneurial journey. We do business to drive sales, but I met some people and built some valuable relationships during this time. It taught me the significance of meticulous planning, flawless execution, sales training, and thorough research in any business endeavor. Moreover, I gained an understanding of the importance of building a robust network and seeking guidance from trusted mentors and industry experts I encountered along the way. The relationships that grew from this experience are priceless. I was able to meet popular YouTubers like 360Jeezy and Evan Carmichael during this time, and it marks one of my best years since opening the Barber Shop.

So, if you harbor an undying passion and an unwavering desire to bring your dreams to life, do not fear taking the leap. But remember to undertake extensive research, plan with precision, and seek counsel from those who have walked the path before you. With unwavering persistence and unrelenting hard work, you can transform your vision into a success.

Shea'd Room

Nyema Tubman and Richelieu Dennis started their journey by selling products made from shea butter sourced from West Africa. They saw an unmet demand in the market for natural and affordable hair care products and created their own brand. They created a wide range of hair and skin care products, including shampoos, conditioners, and styling products using natural and sustainable ingredients. The brand uses plant-based ingredients, like shea butter, coconut oil, and aloe vera, to create products that are gentle on the skin and hair.

Today, Shea Moisture is one of the leading hair and skincare brands in the market, and its founders, Nyema and Richelieu, are recognized as two of the most successful entrepreneurs in the beauty industry. Their story is a testament to the power of perseverance and determination, and it inspires anyone looking to start their own business in the beauty industry.

The company was founded in 1991 in Harlem, New York. In 2017, Shea Moisture was acquired by Johnson & Johnson for a reported $100 million! The acquisition was seen as a strategic move to expand its presence in the growing natural hair and skincare market. Shea Moisture's brand value was estimated to be around $700 million at the time of acquisition.

Shea Moisture's acquisition by Johnson & Johnson was seen as a significant moment in the natural hair industry, as it marked the first time a major multinational corporation had invested in a natural hair and skincare brand. Shea Moisture's founders saw the acquisition as an opportunity to further their mission of empowering communities by making natural and culturally authentic personal care products more accessible to a wider audience.

The acquisition has also helped Shea Moisture to expand its product offerings and reach a broader customer base. The company has continued to grow and maintain its position as a leader in the natural hair and skincare market, and its products are now sold in more than 60 countries worldwide.

U.N.I.T.Y.

In the ever-evolving world of barbering, there is one crucial element that holds the key to unlocking your true potential—the power of self-awareness. Understanding oneself is not just an idle concept; it is the foundation upon which success is built. Allow me to share my journey and the invaluable lessons I've learned about the importance of knowing oneself.

"The most important person to believe in is you. Everyone

else who believes in you means nothing unless if you finally believe in yourself."- Patrick Bet-David

These words reverberate with a profound truth. To thrive in this industry—or any other—you must first comprehend who you are, what drives you, and the unique strengths you possess. This self-awareness becomes the fuel that propels you towards increased productivity, skill elevation, and ultimately, a substantial income.

In my early days, I believed I had it all figured out. I attended conferences, read books, and watched countless YouTube videos, thinking I had gleaned all the knowledge necessary for success. But it was a chance encounter with Marilyn, a seasoned mentor, that shattered my illusion of knowing it all. Marilyn had built and sold several businesses, and her insights proved to be a game-changer.

During our first meeting, I realized that true self-awareness involves acknowledging our strengths and weaknesses. It necessitates being honest with ourselves, even when the truth may sting. I had witnessed far too many barbers deceive themselves, boasting about being the best while struggling to fill their schedules. It became evident that such self-deception hindered growth and stifled progress. To truly excel, we must face our shortcomings head-on and take proactive steps towards improvement. You can't lie to yourself.

Marilyn's wisdom and guidance shed light on a significant

disparity I overlooked within my industry. While many thought leaders focused solely on cutting techniques, there was a lack of emphasis on the business aspects of running a shop and cultivating a loyal clientele. Recognizing this gap, I made a conscious decision to prioritize the business of barbering, fully aware that success extends beyond technical skills alone. I delved deep into developing a thriving shop, nurturing lasting client relationships, and ensuring an exceptional experience for both barbers and customers.

The journey towards self-awareness requires critical thinking, a comprehensive understanding of personal goals, and an unwavering evaluation of where you stand in your career life cycle. It necessitates shedding the fear and doubt that stems from societal conditioning and outdated cultural norms. As I embarked on manifesting my own vision, I realized the paramount importance of aligning my actions with my true aspirations, unswayed by external pressures.

A crucial aspect of this process is seeking counsel from trusted mentors and experts. However, it is imperative to discern the difference between those who possess genuine authority and those who merely claim it. Seek guidance from individuals who have earned their stripes, and who can speak from a position of authority rooted in experience and success. These mentors will empower you to make informed decisions and navigate the path towards greatness. The power of self-awareness cannot be overstated. It is the compass that guides you through the tumultuous waters of this industry, helping you steer clear of distractions and focus on what truly matters. You! By embarking on this journey of self-discovery, you will unlock the door to your own greatness, realizing your full potential and transforming your dreams into reality. Embrace the power of self-awareness as a catalyst that propels you towards a thriving career and rewarding life for you, your loved ones, your team, and your clients.

TRIANGLE OFFENSE

I'm not Black, I'm OJ" - Jay-Z

Seeking success through righteous means, I embarked on a journey of personal growth and self-improvement, which led to the success of Fade in Full. Overcoming challenges like incarceration, substance abuse, and obesity fueled my competitive spirit to achieve more. Scaling our business from a 3-chair shop to a 6-chair shop in a better neighborhood was just the beginning. The next step was to replicate this success. Exploring options, I considered acquiring an existing barbershop for improvement rather than opening a new one.

During my search, I received a call from a man named Mafia Mike, who claimed to have a shop for sale. Intrigued by the opportunity, I agreed to meet him at his office. The encounter raised doubts, with blinds closed on every window and a seemingly empty building. However, I persisted and was welcomed inside by an older woman. After a brief wait, I finally met Mafia Mike, a seasoned businessman with a raspy voice and an Italian accent. He presented himself as a knowledgeable broker in the industry and shared his experience of helping people buy and sell businesses.

Mafia Mike offered me the chance to purchase a shop located next to a popular restaurant. Intrigued, I agreed to visit the location. Arriving at the shop, I found it tucked away in a mixed-use building behind the restaurant. The interior revealed a somewhat outdated and dimly lit space. The chairs showed signs of wear and tear, and the overall ambiance lacked new character. However, I could still envision its potential. Mafia Mike touted the shop's performance, claiming it generated over $100,000 in annual revenue. He mentioned that the owner, Steve, wanted to sell the business due to personal reasons and was looking for a quick exit. The price he quoted, $20,000, seemed unbelievably low, raising questions in my mind.

To gather more information, I met with Steve, the owner, at the shop. I was greeted by an older gentleman giving a haircut to another older man. The atmosphere was tense, with the barber feeling disrupted by my presence. After the customer left, I introduced myself and engaged in a conversation with Steve. He explained his reasons for selling the shop, including his back pain from standing all these years. However, he assured me that the barber currently working there, Tom, would stay if I purchased the shop. Seeking further clarity, I requested a meeting involving Tom, Steve, and the landlord. During the meeting, it became evident that Tom was resistant to change and showed no intention of staying if I took over. Tensions escalated between Tom and Steve, complicating the situation even more. Despite the setbacks, I remained determined and tried to negotiate with Tom, emphasizing the potential for collaboration and improvement.

However, my efforts to reach an agreement with Tom proved futile. He abruptly barred me from the shop and terminated any potential deal, leaving me without a clear explanation. It was a disappointing outcome after months of work and anticipation.

Months later, I discovered that the Main Barbershop, the shop under consideration, was no longer available. The landlord had different plans for the space, signaling a missed opportunity for all pirates involved. Steve would've gotten his severance pay, the landlord would have a new tenant, Tom would've been able to move up from just a barber, and I would've had social proof my systems work for any shop. It was disheartening to think that closed-mindedness and potential prejudices may have played a role in the denial of our opportunity.

Despite the setbacks, I remained resilient and focused on the next endeavor. The experience taught me valuable lessons about navigating the business world, evaluating opportunities, and dealing with unexpected challenges. I was determined to continue seeking growth and success in the barber industry, never losing sight of the ultimate goal: Expansion.

Digi Scale

Expanding from a sole proprietorship to a full-fledged business was a significant milestone for us at Fade in Full Barbershop. We started our journey in a modest 700-square-foot space with just three chairs available for booth rent. As our client base grew and demand increased, we realized the need to expand our operations to accommodate more barbers and provide better services to our customers. This led us to move to a larger 1200-square-foot location, allowing us to establish a six-chair commission shop.

Choosing the right neighborhood for our expansion was crucial. We conducted thorough research and analysis to identify areas with a high population density, a diverse customer base, and limited competition from other barbershops. By targeting neighborhoods that align with our target demographic, we could increase our chances of attracting a steady flow of clients.

When it came to selecting the barbers to join our team, we looked for individuals who shared our passion for the craft and demonstrated a strong work ethic. It was essential to build a team of barbers who could collaborate effectively, support one another's growth, and contribute to the positive culture of our shop. We fostered a sense of camaraderie and teamwork, encouraging open communication and mutual respect among our barbers.

Creating and nurturing a positive culture within our barbershop was instrumental in our success. We emphasized the importance of professionalism, customer service, and continuous learning. We held regular team meetings, training sessions, and workshops to enhance our barbers' skills and keep them updated with the latest trends, quality training, and techniques. By maintaining a supportive and uplifting environment, we ensured that everyone in our shop felt valued and motivated to excel.

Marketing played a pivotal role in our growth strategy. We recognized the need to promote our shop effectively to attract new clients and retain existing ones. We invested in various marketing channels, including social media, local advertising, and community outreach. Word-of-mouth referrals from satisfied customers also played a significant role in our expansion. We constantly sought feedback from our clients and made adjustments to improve their experience.

Managing the financial aspects of our business was a challenge that required careful attention. We secured loans to fund our expansion and invested in the necessary equipment, furniture, and renovations. We implemented efficient bookkeeping practices to track expenses, revenues, and profitability. This enabled us to make informed decisions and allocate resources effectively.

Leadership was a fundamental aspect of our growth. As the business owner, I took on the responsibility of guiding and inspiring our team. I strived to lead by example, demonstrating a strong work ethic, professionalism, and dedication to excellence. Effective leadership ensured that our vision and values were upheld throughout our expansion, creating a sense of unity and purpose among our staff.

Throughout this journey, I remained grounded and never lost touch with what it meant to be a barber. I understood the importance of maintaining my skills, staying connected with clients, and keeping up with industry trends. By staying actively involved in the craft three days a week, I could lead by example and inspire our barbers to continuously strive for excellence while still effectively handling administrative tasks.

While navigating the challenges of expansion, we encountered individuals who didn't share our vision and actively worked against our growth. We faced limiting beliefs, intentional sabotage, and negative influences. Fuck them! We remained steadfast in our goals and stayed the course, believing in our vision for Fade in Full Barbershop. These obstacles only strengthened our resolve to succeed and taught us valuable lessons about resilience, perseverance, and the importance of surrounding ourselves with positive and like-minded individuals.

As we continue to grow, we are committed to maintaining a balance between the business side and the essence of being a barber. We strive to provide an exceptional customer experience while also focusing on the strategic aspects of running a successful barbershop. Our dedication to both the craft and the business allows us to create a thriving and fulfilling environment for both our barbers and our clients. By keeping a strong connection to the barbering profession, we ensure that our services are of the highest quality available and that we stay in touch with the evolving needs and preferences of our clientele. We believe that being hands-on and actively participating in the barbering process allows us to maintain authenticity and provide an unparalleled level of service before the robots take over. By staying connected to the craft, we can lead our team effectively. As a business owner, I have to maintain foresight and understand the challenges, techniques, and trends within the industry. By staying knowledgeable and up-to-date, we can guide our barbers, offer mentorship, and provide the necessary support to help them thrive in their careers. This approach may differ with personality types in the shop. Regardless of origin, a positive and empowering environment within our shop, where our barbers can grow both professionally and personally, is what attracts them to us.

Remaining connected to the barbering profession helps us connect with our clients on a deeper level. We understand the unique needs and expectations of individuals seeking our services, and we can tailor our offerings accordingly. By being involved in the day-to-day operations of the shop, we can build relationships with our clients, provide personalized recommendations, and ensure that their experiences are exceptional.

It's a weekly challenge to remain committed to growth while not losing touch with what it means to be a barber. The authenticity, quality, and customer-centric focus of our Barbershop can be lost with numbers, projections, and profits. By balancing the business side of operations with our passion for the craft, we can create an environment that benefits both our team and our clients, fostering growth, satisfaction, and success.

PROTECT AND SERVE

"People will forget what you said. They will forget what you did. But they will never forget how you made them feel."

- Maya Angelou

What type of Barber are you?

1. **The Player**

   Attracts a lot of baby mamas, good with kids, active in the nightlife—available late afternoons and nights.

2. **The Business Man**

   On time. Charging premium price, late nights, and anything outside of shop hours is considered overtime and charged accordingly. Rarely does walkins; keeps a consistent flow of clients.

3. **The Hustler**

   Cuts fast. In and out of the shop all day, has another source of income, take anyone anytime, and may compromise on price and give out credit cuts.

4. **The Chill Barber**

   Comfortable just getting whatever comes, moving at their own pace, and happy to be doing what they love. Professionals, and not aggressively looking for new clients.

5. **The Entrepreneur**

   Always on the grind, self-promoting, and bringing awareness to themself and the shop. Knows how to advertise, and hands out cards. They like to network, spread the word, and will speak to everyone in the shop even other peoples clients.

6. **The Journey Man**

   Just trying it out. This type may be between jobs; they are reliable, spends time at the shop with a moderate skill level, figuring out if the barber game is for them. May be using the money to fund another project outside of the shop.

7. **The Gossiper**

   Bring in the salon vibes. Talks about other people, spreads rumors, and might hate on other people in the shop to make themselves look better.

8. **The Social Media Influencer**

   Attract attention online. Makes youtube videos, shorts, and Tik tok. Makes tutorials and review tools, stays up to date on trends, and even sets some. They also do the enhancements and have a strong online presence.

9. **The OG**

   The elder statesman of the shop; has life experience,

and provides wisdom and stability. Breaks up fights and arguments; usually the judge and jury of an internal conflict in the shop.

Shut Up and Cut

Have you ever watched ESPN First Take and heard people complain about how athletes should JUST play the game?!

Of course, we want them to play their best and win. However, they're people like we are; they live in the world and experience reality with us. Our exposure to certain injustices or life events may be relative; however, they have thoughts and emotions too, just like us. They aren't robots. Throughout time we've seen some polarizing athletes and thought leaders within the sports world.

If they only played the game, how would we view LeBron, Muhammad Ali, Kobe, Tyson, or even Colin Kaepernik? Our personality, views, and opinions shape who we are at the core and set us apart from the rest. Early in my barber career, I was so intimidated by the actual process of doing the haircut that I failed to engage with my customers. My cheat code was blasting the music and getting lost in the art of the cut, and it worked for years, tbh. However, I didn't know much about my people, and they didn't know much about me. At that time, I still relied on walk-ins, so when it was slow, I didn't have contact info for follow ups or any leads. Hope is not a strategy.

One common thing I noticed about the Barbers that came before me is that they always acknowledged their clients by name when they walked through the door. Even now, I visit other barbershops,

169

and people immediately speak to their people by name when they walk in. If not the name, they reference a running joke. - Anything that builds rapport. Everyone isn't gonna wanna talk or be friendly, and that's all good. Everything isn't for everyone. One thing for sure I've seen is Barbers become well-known and successful with subpar skills because they have personality and charisma.

Client love languages

1. **APPRECIATION**

   "I know I can count on you."

   "Thank you for trusting me with your hair."

   Showing appreciation to your clients is extremely valuable. It helps build a positive and long-lasting relationship, shows that you value their business, and helps to retain clients. A simple gesture of appreciation, such as a thank you card or a small gift, can go a long way in making your clients feel appreciated and valued. Moreover, a positive reputation through word of mouth is one of the best forms of advertising and is directly influenced by the way you treat your clients. So, showing appreciation to your clients not only improves their experience with your business, but it can also drive new business your way.

2. **RECOGNITION**

   "You're reliable."

   "You're consistent."

   Showing recognition to your clients can be a valuable way of showing love and building a strong relationship with them. By acknowledging their loyalty and support, you are expressing your gratitude and reinforcing their decision to choose your services. This can also lead to increased customer satisfaction, repeat business, and positive word-of-mouth recommendations, which can benefit your business in the long run.

3. LISTENING

Listening and asking the right questions makes your client feel important, and builds trust and rapport. Listening can be considered as a love language for clients. When a barber takes the time to listen to their client's needs and preferences, it shows that they value their opinions and care about the end result. This creates a strong sense of trust and appreciation between the barber and the client, which can lead to a long-lasting and loyal relationship. By actively listening and paying attention to their client's concerns, a barber can also make sure that they are providing the best possible service, which is a key component of building a successful business in the hair and beauty industry.

4. CHALLENGE

Whenever your clients speak about an achievement or goal, be a source of encouragement for them. Challenging clients can be effective in certain situations, but it's important to approach it in a way that is respectful, supportive, and constructive. If done well, challenging clients can help them grow and improve, leading to greater satisfaction and stronger relationships. However, if done poorly, challenging clients can be perceived as negative and may harm the relationship. It's important to understand the individual client's needs, preferences, and communication style, and to approach the challenge in a way that is tailored to their needs and is perceived as positive and supportive.

5. **CONNECTIONS**

Your client base serves as a network of contacts that helps you, and they can also help one another. For example, if you have a client looking for a house and another client who is a real estate agent, and you link these two, you're forever a key contributor to both parties and that increases your value. Being a connector of people means you need to be a good judge of character. Be a connector of individuals that genuinely have good intentions.

Every day won't be easy in this business. I've been a barber for decades now, and one of my biggest fears is an empty schedule. On a January evening, I checked my Saturday appointments and saw that I only had three; my heart sank. My mind, always quick to respond with emotions before logic, started racing. What did I do wrong? Did I mess up some cuts? Was I not present enough? Was I charging too much? My first weekend of the year was dead. Most barbers would simply brush it off, but not me. I've remained hungry, always pushing forward. To make sense of things, I decided to check my stats for the first three weeks of January for the past few years. To my disappointment, this recent one was the worst. So, I took action. I grabbed some blank greeting cards and wrote to all my clients that I hadn't seen in a while. I called them, letting them know I had something for them. Some eventually came in to grab the cards, so the results were mixed. Some were affected by the blizzard or simply struggling after the holiday season, but my persistence paid off. I learned that even in the toughest of times, there's always a way to keep pushing forward.

RETENTION

"If you ain't got the clientele say hell no, cause they gon want they money rain, sleet hail snow"
- Notorious BIG

Ask most barbers how many heads they cut in a week., and most likely, they'll say, "I think like," "somewhere around" or "maybe" not quite knowing the exact number. That was me at one time. Coming up in booth rent shops, I was only focusing on the money more than the actual service. Relying on walk-ins meant we sat around aimlessly and waited; watched movies, TV shows, and watched the established barbers get busy or stand outside and stop everyone that walked by. So whenever we had a rush of people in the shop, we literally had to rush! Get through the cut as fast as possible to get everyone you can get. I'm thankful for those times because they helped me with speed; however, I sacrificed quality and precision. At some point, as a barber, you'll want to build up a solid client base once you have the skills down, and here's the key; Retention!

How do you retain people? Who do you want to retain?

First, you need to know what kind of barber you want to be to qualify for the type of clients you want. There is no such thing as the perfect barber. We all have unique strengths or weaknesses. One thing I know for sure is that we attract what we are for the most part. If you want people to respect your schedule and be on time, then you have to do the same for them. If you want people to tip and pay for premium service, then you have to provide that to them. If you want them to offer you value and referrals, you have to do just the same. For a long time, I didn't really talk to people much because my conversation was limited. Being in shops where we blasted the music and debated all day was where I learned about the technical skill of cutting hair. Once I became a little more mature and wanted more, I started to talk to my clients more- understanding their needs and goals outside of just the haircut. Building a lasting relationship with a client takes some work- remembering names, details and actually being interested in them. Along my barber journey, I noticed that there were barbers with average skill level killing it with clients because they had charisma and personality. Most people in the community see the Barbershop as a place to talk and decompress, so if you're able to provide that type of environment in addition to a good quality cut, you'll be able to keep them.

Now, there are no end-all strategies to being more personable. I suggest being the best version of you is the way to go. Be polite, speak, smile, and listen. Whatever is going on outside, leave it outside. If your customer is happy, great; if they are going through

QUALITY > QUANTITY

Do you want more people paying average prices or fewer people paying high prices?

I've been blessed to say I've experienced both; 18-hour days at $15-$20 cuts to 6-hour days of $60 cuts, and I prefer the 6-hour day. Cutting 30 people in a day made sense while I was in survival mode, now that I have the status, I could ease up. Most barbers I talk to DON'T WANT TO RAISE PRICES. Building relationships with people can get blurred between friends and business. If you're in high demand and burning out, nobody's gonna feel sorry for you, and a few will offer you more money. It's clearly time to raise the price. What are we scared of? Losing people?! It's gonna happen regardless. This is something we have to accept about the game. Any customers that are chasing a low price aren't really your client.

Customers are people you cut for the first time, and clients are people you retain over time. Don't devalue your time. Don't devalue your service and business for anyone. Since I've struggled with pricing for myself and in the shop, I've created a framework to raise prices based on stats.

Retaining clients is more important than attracting new ones once you are going strong in Barbering. A high retention rate shows your value in the marketplace, and a full schedule of appointments is an indication of high demand. As a result, you can raise your prices and increase your income. There are only three ways to increase income as a barber: charge more, cut your operating costs, or create a new revenue stream through new products or services. The key to success is consistency and providing quality services every time.

To provide a quality experience for clients, focus on the stages of your service: the opening, consultation, actual service, and the close. During the opening, greet the client and remember their name or something about their previous appointment. The consultation should minimize options and fully understand the client's desired look. The service should be a light convo or narrated, explaining each step and using products to educate clients on the benefits of hair care. Finally, the close should paint a picture of how the cut has improved the client's life.

During the close, you'll have a chance to retain clients; you should aim to rebook and ask for reviews and referrals. A wise man once told me that you keep a schedule full by filling the schedule. I'll be honest, when I was at my peak, it was annoying to rebook people after their haircut. I would be thinking, why are we concerned about two weeks from now when I have another person ready to hop in my chair right now?! That minute or so to put someone in my schedule for later is the reason why I'd stay busy while the other barbers were sitting around. Why not rebook them? It's literally the best way to claim a client as yours. A full schedule of appointments shows high demand for you, and it can indicate to increase the service price. By focusing on the quality experience for clients, barbers can increase referrals and maintain consistent income.

For a while, I was calculating retention by how much a percentage are booked appointments vs the total number of services for a month. If you have above 70% appointments as a barber, then you are doing well. If a barber has 100% appointments with no room for a walk-in or a last-minute person, they ain't charging enough; I've had arguments with barbers over this. One came to me complaining about money and was booked all day, every day. He wanted me to increase his commission split, and I told him to increase his PRICE. "Charge those people that are booking you out more!" I said. I get the concept of cutting costs but decreased split or booth rent still leaves you with the same workload for the same money. A better approach is to raise the price, let the cheapos drop off, and you can make the same or more for less physical damage to your body.

Don't get high on your own supply

Relying on walk-ins is not the wave for an established barber. If you are reading this and you have been in the game for a while, why are you doing this to yourself? If you're a walk-in type guy at a walk-in type shop, then that's fine; you chose your path. However, if you accept appointments, are available on a scheduling app, and are an 'established' personality in your shop and you never have appointments, then something is wrong! Walk-ins are most likely the shop's clients. If you are in demand, then people will book you. I say all of this to share a story with you about a barber that was killing it, doing well, and making money on walk-ins. I explained to him that if he were able to get a majority of his people to book with him that he should raise his price. So he started to mark all his walk-ins as appointments, inflating his stats. Knowing this, I advised him to keep his price the same. He took it upon himself to raise his price anyway. He didn't raise it to a fair market price for a skilled and professional barber; he almost doubled his price! Now he just sits there and waits for walk-ins. Nobody is booking at all. Why? Well, if you are the top dog, people will know, respect, and pay what you are worth. You can set a price however you like it, but if you aint worth it, nobody is paying it.

There is a guy whose ads I keep seeing on youtube advertising a course to get barbers to charge more for cuts. The ads are well scripted, and they should target me, so I'd say they are executed very well. However, while I was speaking to some younger barbers, they asked me about it and my thoughts. I've already given you my formula on prices here, so I can't speak to this online course without taking it. I will say this: If these online gurus have a strategy to get you up to $250 for a haircut in your mom's garage, then by all means, you need to check out that course. If you don't love this profession yet you are good at it, and you don't depend on it for your living, then maybe you should charge a high price so you don't have to cut hair as often and money can motivate you to do it. I am not ever gonna tell you to cheat yourself. Get your money; just know your worth. A focus on quality experience and retention will increase the barber's value in the market and lead to higher prices and increased income.

Pillars of Quality Control

1. **Appreciate the Customer**

   I should rephrase this to appreciate the customers that appreciate you! They can go anywhere, and they are choosing you.

2. **Ensure tools and workspace is clean**

   I know we're not rocking dirty tools and stations this late in this book. Come on, fam; act as if this is your house. Would you really have people over and your place is a mess?. Having dirty tools maybe worst than that. The last thing you want is someone catching a disease from your dirty tools. Keep your shit clean!

3. **Uphold the shop rules and values**

   Every shop has it's own rules and culture. Keep it consistent while being open to upgrades and new ideas. All ideas should come with a "who" & "how" so you can execute and stay creative.

4. **Improve forever**

I cant stress this one enough; self improvement and learning is essential. Everyone is on this same type of time, and you have a team destined for greatness.

SUPPORT

"What do we live for if not to make life less difficult for each other?"

– George Eliot, Novelist

Lean Back

On a random day, as I scrolled through Instagram, I stumbled upon a video that resonated deeply with me—a message about healthcare for low-income individuals. Compelled to share it, I reposted the video and tagged the person behind it. To my surprise, I received a direct message from none other than Fat Joe himself; Don Cartagena! This was the real deal—the same artist I had passionately supported in my barbershop during our rap debates. I had created playlists of his music and vibed with him since the 90s!

The rapper within me couldn't resist the opportunity, so I asked for a verse. After all, he had reached out to me. However, his response brought me back down to earth. He quoted a price of

185

50k for a verse! We engaged in negotiations, but we couldn't find common ground, and our conversation eventually went cold. Initially, I was frustrated, but then I took a moment to reflect on how much I truly knew about Joe. He wasn't just a rapper; he was a businessman, philanthropist, husband, and father, among other things. There were so many other things I could have asked for.

I could have inquired about opening one of his sneaker stores in Western New York. I could have requested mentorship or connections. I could have asked him to repost my music video or promote our barbershop on social media. At that moment, I realized that my perception of Joe was limited to my initial impression—a rapper, and it made me think about how others might perceive me. Many of my clients knew little about my life beyond their haircuts. Some were even unaware that I owned the shop!

This experience taught me that people tend to latch onto a single vision of who they think you are, regardless of your growth. However, there are millionaires and billionaires who shatter this narrow perspective within minutes of meeting them. When they are asked what they do, they respond with a simple question: "What do you need?" At that moment, they position themselves as authorities and helpers. Your response determines the direction of the relationship moving forward.

We are more than just barbers; we are business people. Our purpose extends beyond providing haircuts—we are in the business of helping others. Most importantly, we are in the business of business. Take a step back, zoom out, and examine yourself and your career. Just like Joe has more to offer than a verse, you have more to offer than a haircut.

Why so serious?!

During my peak years as a barber, I had the incredible opportunity to cut the hair of notable individuals like French Montana and Stevie Johnson, among others. These connections were established through relationships, and I was able to demonstrate my skills to maintain those relationships.

One particular moment that boosted my credibility was when Stevie gave me a shout-out for his haircut on ESPN's First Take. It was an exhilarating experience for me. Although we weren't an exceptionally strong team at that time, we had a dedicated fan base, and he was the star of the show. Being his barber opened doors to cutting other players, and when I connected with Aaron Maybin, he provided significant financial support during a much-needed period. Sometimes, he would generously pay $200 for a single cut, and he always had additional clients at his place who were willing to pay as well. One of the people I met during that time, Alex Carrington, remains a loyal client to this day.

While I was cutting the Buffalo Bills players and working at the barbershop, I was also hustling in the streets, selling mixtapes. I rarely took breaks to enjoy life, working relentlessly and being careless with my finances. This eventually led me to hit a few dead ends. My car broke down, CD sales declined, I had a falling out with my DJ, and I found myself entangled in rap beefs and other complications.

During this low point, I spent time with a fellow barber who was relatively new to the game but had been a close friend for years. He was older and experienced, so I trusted his judgment. Unfortunately, he used all the challenges I was facing as ammunition to motivate me. He would say things like, "If that's your man, he should be helping you." Regrettably, I allowed him to fuel my ambition, leading me to ask Stevie for money to open my own shop immediately after he signed his contract. Ignoring my gut feeling, I thought, "What do I have to lose?" Well, I lost the relationship. Stevie didn't give me a strong objection, but before I knew it, I saw him getting a haircut from another barber on Instagram. Our relationship was never the same, and I didn't help matters with drunken tweets and negative energy during that period.

I didn't intend to discuss this incident here, but it's relevant because Stevie recently appeared on a podcast where he was asked about me, and apparently, he didn't remember me. We haven't spoken in years. Perhaps he forgot, maybe my name was mentioned incorrectly, or perhaps what I did was truly unforgivable. I didn't need this incident to know that what I did was wrong. I haven't had an opportunity to apologize or provide an explanation, if one was even necessary. Since then, I've moved on and successfully opened my own shop, which has allowed me to transform my life. I'm now on a different path compared to back then, and I've learned invaluable lessons along the way:

- Trust your instincts and avoid listening to people who don't have your best interests at heart.
- Clients have the freedom to choose any barber, so maintaining relationships is crucial.
- I should have addressed my drinking habits much earlier, as they caused damage to important relationships.
- Start a business with my own capital and develop a solid business plan before seeking financial assistance. Back then, I lacked the business experience I have now, and my timing was terrible. Many others were likely asking for money right after Stevie signed his contract. I made myself a liability instead of an asset. The barber he chose already owned his shop and had more in common with him than I did.
- Cutting hair for celebrities has its advantages and disadvantages. While I was grateful for the opportunity, I found that they often had demanding expectations, and I couldn't always attend to my regular clients while chasing after them. Additionally, some celebrities didn't pay top dollar for me to pack up my tools and travel to their homes or training camps in Rochester, NY, where I would sometimes earn less than I would at the shop. At that time, I prioritized the relationship over the money, but eventually, I realized the importance of valuing my skills and time appropriately, especially when I needed

the income.

These experiences have shaped me and taught me valuable lessons about trust, relationships, business, and self-worth.

The other side of the game

Nobody loves the dark side unless you're Kobe, Jordan, or Mayweather. Have you ever thought about what drives them to compete on the highest level? Better yet, have you ever thought about what drives you? Starting a business requires that same level of focus, dedication, and consistency if you want to thrive. Starting as self-employed and relying on your talent requires a championship work ethic. Low barriers of entry type businesses are challenging to scale to billions and don't look sexy to VC firms or Wall Street investors. The amount of sacrifice poured into Fade in Full with dreams to be better than Super Cuts has strained close relationships along the way. It stressed bank accounts, personal lives, and tested sanity. A life-changing decision occurred in November 2015 and on December 11th, 2015, ink was drying on my first LLC. Renting a booth as a worker didn't require finding commercial space, searching for equipment, building teams, or being responsible for helping others make money—leaders eat last. Most founders start a business without those details mapped out. They think profits come fast and go to the top guy. It might be true for a Fortune 500 corporation or unicorn tech startup, not for a Barbershop.

They say if you wanna hide something, put it in a book. I won't spare the bloody details here and sell a dream like this path was cheesecake. This entrepreneurial leap was a nose dive from a business partnership that didn't end well. While "owning" that partner shop, I grieved three deaths, caught 2 DWIs, and ended up back in the drug game to fund lawyers and fines. Not quite where I wanted to be in my mid 30s. Instead of responding to it like an emotionally intelligent adult, I handled it like a broken clock.— right twice a day. Substance abuse, partying excessively, and womanizing were my medicine. My girlfriend at the time was a clean cut good girl from the south, and I was an Eastside Buffalo guy with issues. She saw potential in me despite failed promises and a lack of discipline. One major flaw was not knowing the power of no. I didn't turn down clients and kept churning cuts to no end. I didn't turn down the party and stayed out all night long. I didn't turn down the drinks and blacked out religiously. The cycle continued for more than half a decade until I hit the bottom.

One Sunday morning, I woke up with a headache that felt like someone had scooped the middle of my brain like ice cream. I crawled up from the floor, not sure how I got there. I felt disgusted having little to show for being 35 and a well-known Barber. Almost 20 years of ups and downs earned me a trash bag of clothes, a mattress on the floor, pills on the dresser, cheap Vodka, and that was it. I'd sold my truck to help fund the Barbershop. I imagined what the younger me would think of this fat nasty broke adult. Who was I fooling? My relationship with the southern girl was shattered. My family knew I was a street-level drug dealer slash barber with failed attempts at rap stardom. The

NFL players that helped me gain notoriety had moved on. Every checking account was in the red, from buying a job (investing in a shop) and drowning in it, getting carried out unconscious after exhausting days, and waking up with empty pockets weekly. I've seen some washed-up barbers along my way, and none quite as fucked up as this. It was my fault, a sum of bad decisions and the average of who I was spending most of my time with.

Those trends came to a screeching halt once I looked into the accountability mirror. The first move to restore my life was to stop drinking. I had never been as determined to do it. Drew, who allowed me to use his spare room, was the first person that I shared my goal with—those first few weeks of sobriety entailed going to the gym when I felt pressure to drink, then 18-hour days became 8 hours at best. I set standards—no more last minute cuts or drinking inside the shop. No more broken thrift store furniture in the shop. No more answering every single notification on my personal phone and being torn from my client to try and fit in more people. I started to think beyond survival mode as a barber and began to mind my business: The shop.

The change introduced new challenges. Working on the business was greater than working in the business. Enforcing rules and protecting my investment revealed how unimportant it was to those that were not accepting of my growth. I tried to hang on as long as I could. I still care about those relationships, although I've moved on.

A community with low degrees of separation doesn't allow room for mistakes—Any flaw, setback, or blemish gets picked apart and viewed with a magnifying glass. People that were close friends become enemies. Wartime leaders may have to take a peaceful position to protect casualties. Saying no to people in order to say yes to you is bad news for the narcissistic, toxic, and manipulative people in your life. Bad news spreads faster; it's human nature. People talk. When you surpass expectations, jealous ones will envy you. Give them more to talk about with living up to your standards and following your dreams. People that are stuck on who you were are dumb, deaf, blind, or scarred.

Life will test you no matter what path you choose. Barbers have the same struggles as any other profession, if not more. Being self-employed will force you to navigate through a jungle with cliffs, vicious animals, and storms. There are frustrating times; like times when you visualize the final result of a great haircut before you have the skills to execute it. Stressing over how you're going to make a living while sitting in a slow shop is a confidence killer. Losing some of your most beloved clients to long jail sentences or death is depressing. I never imagined that being a barber would force me to make critical decisions, make sacrifices, or get hurt by people that I genuinely wanted to help.

Traditional 9-5 jobs offer benefits and stability. In the Barber game, you have to create that and more for yourself one way or another. The perfect situation does not exist. The only thing that is certain is that you have to dedicate yourself to giving max effort in a competitive space, find the best opportunity, leverage it, and pivot in tough times. Most of us know what not to do, yet we fall into bad patterns from time to time. All of us have bad patterns relative to our lives.

Expect to show up on days when you really don't want to be there. Be ready to dread the minutes and hours of exposure to some of your customers and how limited their thinking may be—remaining mute through conversations that kill your brain cells. I've seen customers get fired by the older barbers when I was on the come-up and didn't understand why. Imagining a better life that feels distant may depend on your perspective. Motivating those around you to pursue more than the minimum isn't for everyone.

Also, having crucial conversations with your co-workers about things they've done that caused your clients to leave you and leave the shop a bad review can be tough. Reaching the status you've been wanting may cause you to question if it was worth it; it comes with back pains, hip issues, biceps tears, and the fear of taking a vacation to hold on to your clients. Servicing the same group for decades is great when they accept you, pay your price, and respect your time. Everyone doesn't have the ability to reason or see from your perspective. They just want what they asked for—a cut. You'll have to be stern in respecting your life & time regardless. Protecting your peace and controlling your destiny by staying aligned with your purpose every day you wake up.

Reading this with a closed mind can be reality-crushing for a young barber or journeyman looking for microwave results. We've all seen barbers that only last for weeks and months, and that was the end, some ended up blaming the owners, criticizing the customers, and leaving the game in denial. Truth is, everyone doesn't have what it takes to be a successful barber. Your will must be stronger than your skill. Great barbers have an "it" factor, and game time will test how much "it" you really got.

With years in, you'll be able to view from a higher frequency, notice trends, evaluate personalities, make tough calls, and handle these tense situations.

BURNOUT

"Burnout is what happens when you try to avoid being human for too long."

~ Michael Gungor

This may not be well received, but it's a wake-up call for people who feel stuck in the same routine. The barber game brought me joy and struggle over the years. I've missed important family events, and my work schedule has negatively impacted my social and love life for decades. Substance abuse was also a problem for me, and I've been through many ups and downs in my career. During the ups, you may make personal sacrifices while chasing the bag, and the downs are dark if you aren't responsible with your health and finances during the ups. Being a barber requires a high level of dedication to self-preservation in order to serve your customers and your shop. I learned to fix myself before serving others over the past few years.

Being a barber became my identity since I was drawn to this

craft as a way to fit in and make money in my neighborhood. My true passion is creation, and I also enjoy making music, editing videos, reading, writing this book, and running my own barbershop. Despite the relationships I've built with my clients and the skills I've gained, the physical and emotional demands of this job have taken a toll. Standing all day with repetitive moves that aren't ergonomically friendly will have your body on fire! Back pain, wrist pain, tendonitis, and hip issues are part of most busy Barbers' ride into the sunset. Also, the range of personalities and conflicts you encounter can be draining at times, leaving you with minimal energy for your loved ones. Not everyone is cut out for the barber game. Many have quit, turned to drugs, and some have even committed suicide. Witnessing this firsthand, in addition to my own patterns was a strong indicator to prioritize my peace of mind.

Despite the challenges, I credit my grandmother, Emma J Bassett, for inspiring me to open up a shop. Since my early teens, she's been telling me that I should have my own shop. I'm also forever appreciative of Uncle BB for giving me a much-needed $1000 when I told him I was going to do it years after she passed away. A few devastating losses hit me hard within a short period of time. My Father, my brother, and my grandmother passed away, and I continued to work during the time I needed to grieve; living self-employed life since 13 conditioned me like that though. What else can you do when you lose the core of your support group while needing to support yourself? Dealing with clients and coworkers who may not always be considerate of your needs or well-being doesn't help either; and to be fair, it's not their responsibility, some will save you once they see you become your own hero. Leaning on yourself to build confidence, trusting in your ability, and stepping out of your comfort zone can lead you to friends and advisors that have your best interests at heart.

Opening a Barbershop brought me joy and hardship. It opened my eyes to more than the self-employed quadrant. Building careers, systems, and providing empowerment to those on the come up is great when you see them grow. Many of my disciples have seen me evolve too. The hardship lies in fierce competition, hiring skilled/reliable barbers, slow seasons, and reputation management. Recruiting new barbers will always be crucial since the turnover can be high. Schools are producing students with licenses but without a clear understanding of the challenges of this job. We need realistic advice that can help to develop a strong support system. There are many groups and organizations nationwide that offer resources. They lobby for regulations within our industry, yet the variance on health care and retirement benefits has left some of us uncertain.

The relentless pace of the barber shop and constant demands can drain you and leave you questioning your passion. We deal with stress in different ways— reigniting your flame may come in the form of prioritizing health care & nutrition. For a long time, I was skipping lunches and eating the bad foods that didn't keep good fuel in the tank. Maintaining a healthy diet keeps your energy up and increases your years of productivity. Another way to refresh is to take some time off if you're able to do so. Even a road trip a few hours away is good. Often I'd just hit the road and visit some cities within four hours of where I live and visit those Barbershops to chop it up with some like-minded people in our industry. Visiting other shops is always inspirational for me because I feel the vibe and energy in a different environment. I may end up upgrading based on what they are doing or coming back appreciating how good we got it! If you have hobbies dive right in and experience those. Throughout my barber career, I've always found other things to do that I enjoy, including visiting conferences and schools. Another one that I've been able to apply to my career is video editing and reading. That's me though, you know what's best for you, could be skydiving for all I know. You shouldn't be a slave to your clippers. Enjoy this game and experience it in a way that makes your life better. Burnout may be inescapable, and if you prioritize self awareness, you will have the tools to bring you back from the deep end. I've been close to the cliff—I had to take a step back several times and moderate my productivity. Turning people down is your right as an independent contractor. Working at a pace that fits your lifestyle is your decision, so you are not alone in this industry. Together we can flourish and handle any challenge that is in our way, create a legacy, and transcend just giving haircuts. Remember that what you do has an impact on people's lives and increases their confidence. You have to take care of yourself so you can take care of your people.

Actionable Steps

1. Self-Awareness and Reflection:
- Take a moment to reflect on your own well-being and identify any signs of burnout or exhaustion.
- Acknowledge the physical and emotional toll that the barbering profession can have on your body and mental health.
- Recognize the importance of self-preservation and finding a balance between work and personal life.

2. Health and Nutrition:
- Prioritize your health by adopting a healthy diet and eating regular, nourishing meals.
- Avoid skipping meals and consuming unhealthy foods that don't provide sustainable energy.
- Consider seeking professional advice on nutrition and creating a meal plan that supports your overall well-being.

3. Time Off and Mental Breaks:
- Allow yourself regular breaks and time off from work to recharge and rejuvenate.
- Plan short getaways or road trips to explore new environments and gain inspiration from other barber shops.
- Engage in hobbies or activities outside of work that bring you joy and help you disconnect from the demands of the profession.

4. Seek Support and Resources:
- Connect with industry groups, organizations, and conferences that offer resources and support for barbers.

- Build a strong support system of like-minded individuals who understand the challenges you face.
- Consider seeking mentorship or guidance from experienced barbers who can provide advice and perspective.

5. Prioritize Boundaries and Self-Care:
- Learn to say no and set boundaries to protect your well-being.
- Understand that taking care of yourself is not selfish; it enables you to provide better service to your clients and maintain long-term success.
- Engage in activities that bring you joy and fulfillment outside of work, allowing yourself time to pursue your passions and interests.

6. Moderate Productivity and Pace:
- Recognize that burnout is inescapable if you consistently push yourself beyond your limits.
- Moderate your productivity and workload to prevent exhaustion and maintain a sustainable pace.
- Learn to prioritize quality over quantity, focusing on providing exceptional service rather than overworking yourself.

NOTES

FINAL THOUGHTS

This book is a testament to what I've learned, what has inspired me, and my journey in the barber game. Despite the cultural challenges, I'm grateful for the opportunities it has given me to have a fair shot at life, meet new people, and learn valuable skills.

Example of Call Script

"Hi, my name is _____ from _____. Thank you for downloading our offer."

Be sure to mention it's a COURTESY CALL and when the offer expires.

The difference between Hot, Warm, & Cold Leads.

HOT = Ready to book/ Already a client

WARM = Been to our shop before but not a full-time client.

COLD= Not interested/ Clueless/ Had a horrible experience with us

NEED TO KNOWS

-Looking for a new Barber

-Looking for a better barbershop

-New to the area

-Knows someone who's already a client

-Already follows us on social media

FAQs from Prospects

Where are you located?

How much do you charge?

Do you cut kids' hair?

Are you open late?

Can you cut straight hair?

Can you cut Black hair?

Are you open on Mondays?

Can you do a Fade?

Can you do a Razor Shave?

Do you clean your clippers?

Are you looking for Barbers?

Do I have to book an appointment?

Can I walk in?

Do you play cursing music in there?

Can you edge up?

Objections & Rebuttals

"MY BARBER CHARGES LESS"

Do you usually make decisions based on low prices, or do you look for overall quality?

Not saying we can match our shop's price; however, if our prices were the same, would you rather do business with us?

"I ALREADY HAVE A BARBER"

I understand you being loyal to your barber. Have we failed to show the difference in value and quality?

"YOU'RE TOO FAR FROM ME"

"I'VE BEEN THERE, AND _____ MESSED ME UP."

"THAT PRICE IS TOO HIGH"

When you say you can't afford it, do you mean you can't afford it now, found a barber charging less, or it's outside your budget?

Or are you just complaining as you do about your bills and paying anyway? Lol

All conversations should lead them to an appointment unless they outrightly say they're not interested or prove to be unqualified. Most people will not give you a hard "no." That's why you ask questions to figure out the situation. Your tonality matters, and you'll need to be patient. Trust me.

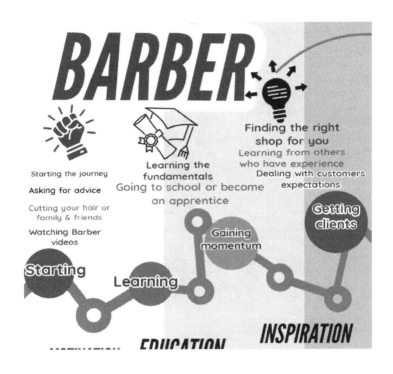

Made in the USA
Columbia, SC
07 October 2023

7e6afa53-c5af-413a-8125-0216a7e08ec3R01